To

From

Published by **Lion Children's Books**
www.lionhudson.com
Part of the SPCK Group
SPCK, 36 Causton Street, London, SW1P 4S

ISBN 978 07459 7928 1 hardback
ISBN 978 0 7459 7929 8 gift hardback

First edition 2021
This edtion 2023

Acknowledgments
Scripture quotations on pages 88–89 are taken from The Holy Bible, New International Bible®, NIV® Copyright © 1973, 1978, 1984, 2011 by Biblica, Inc.® Used by permission. All rights reserved worldwide.

A catalogue record for this book is available from the British Library

Printed and bound in China, September 2022, LH54

The Lion *Wondrous* BIBLE

Retold by Deborah Lock
Illustrated by Alida Massari

LION CHILDREN'S

Contents

THE OLD TESTAMENT 10

The Wonder of Creation 12
The Garden 15
The Tempting Fruit 15
The Separation 17
The Great Flood 18
The Rainbow Promise 20
The Tower of Confusion 23
A Man Chosen 24
A Second Covenant 26
Hagar's Child 28
The Laughing Son 28
The Test of Sacrifice 30
The Birthright 32
A Lesson Learned 33
A Return Home 35
Dreams of Greatness 38
Taken to Egypt 40
Imprisoned 41
Pharaoh's Dreams 42
The Famine 44

A Family Reunion 46
A Baby Saved 47
The Burning Bush 50
The Plagues 52
Exodus 53
The Ten Commandments 56
The Tabernacle 59
The Spies 61
Balaam's Donkey 62
Entering the Promised Land 64
The Fall of Jericho 66
The Time of the Judges 68
Ruth, the Faithful Daughter-in-Law 71
Samuel, Born to Serve 74
A Prophetic Calling 75
Israel's First King 78
The Shepherd Boy 80
Slaying a Giant 81
A Faithful Friendship 84
Psalms of King David 86
Moments of Kindness and Weakness 90
The Wisdom of King Solomon 92
Jerusalem's Temple 94

A Divided Kingdom 96
Elijah the Prophet 98
The Voice in the Silence 100
Naboth's Vineyard 101
Stories of Elisha 103
The Healing of Naaman 105
Jonah, the Reluctant Prophet 107
A City Saved 109
King Josiah's Reforms 110
The Fall of Jerusalem 112
Exiled in Babylon 114
The Lions' Den 117
The Return from Exile..119
Esther, the Chosen Queen 121
The Courageous Request 123

THE NEW TESTAMENT 126
A Promised King 128
Chosen Parents 131
A Humble Birth 134
Presented in the Temple 139
The Guiding Star 140
In My Father's House 144
John the Baptist 145
Tempted 147
In the Synagogue 148
Calling the First Disciples 149
The Wedding at Cana 152
Choosing the Twelve 153
Blessings 155
The Lord's Prayer 158
The Centurion's Faith 159
The Story of the Sower 161
Calming the Storm 162
"Little Girl, Get Up!" 165
Feeding the 5,000 168
On the Mountain 171
The Good Samaritan 173
The Rich Man and the Poor Man 177

The Least and the Lost 179
Blessing the Children 180
The Last Will Be First 182
Martha and Mary 184
"Lazarus, Come Out!" 186
The Expensive Perfume 187
The Triumphant Entry 188
At the Temple 190
The Last Meal 192
Betrayal 195
Denial 196
Sentenced to Death 198
At the Cross 201
The Stone Tomb 204
Arisen and Alive! 206
The Walk to Emmaus 208
Doubts and Belief 209
Breakfast on the Beach 211
Return to Heaven 212
Wind and Flames 214
In the Name of Jesus 217
Brave Stephen 219
Good News Spreads 220

A Blinding Light 221
"Tabitha, Get Up!" 224
Paul's First Journey 226
New Disciples in Greece..228
The Night in Prison 230
Riots and Arrest 233
Sent to Rome 236
Shipwrecked! 237
Paul's Letters 239
John's Vision 242
The Glory of Heaven 244
The Wonder of a New Creation 248
Index of People's Names 252

THE BIBLE IS a collection of books full of wonder and wondrous stories. The books are split into two parts. The Old Testament is the first part, with thirty-nine books. These were written by many different people over hundreds of years. The types of writing are varied and include historical accounts, poetry, laws, wise sayings, warnings and hopes, and stories full of meaning. The word "Testament" means an agreement or covenant. The "Old" part tells the story of God's covenant with people of his chosen nation. Things did not always go smoothly; people went their own way instead of following God's path. But within the Old Testament, there are many wonderful moments when God's power is revealed.

The Old Testament

The Wonder of Creation

Genesis 1–2

All was formless and dark in the beginning. The mighty and powerful wind of God swept over this endless, timeless void. Then the very first wonder happened. A commanding word of God broke through the silence, saying, "Let there be light." Light filled the emptiness.

God began to create order by separating the light of day from the dark of night. God formed the sky and then brought together the waters into oceans so that areas of dry land appeared. God began to create life as plants grew and flowered and produced fruit with seeds for new ones to grow. The earth flourished with an abundance of many varieties of plants. During the day the sun shone in the sky, and at night the moon shimmered and stars twinkled through the dark. God saw that what had been created was good.

The life-giving word of God continued to speak, saying, "Let there be living creatures in the waters and in the sky." The first animals swam through the oceans and those with wings flew in the air. God blessed them, and the sea creatures and birds produced many offspring, filling the earth. Then God made a great variety of animals to live on the land, creeping and leaping, grazing and chattering. From the mountains to the valleys, the world was filled with every kind of animal.

But God had not finished creating yet. The loving word of God spoke once again, saying, "I will make human beings to love, care, and provide as I do. I will bless them and they will flourish. They will look after all the animals that I have made and keep the world in order. They will eat the fruits of the plants that I have provided." Now everything was very good and so God rested, blessing the day as a special time to enjoy all that was wonderfully created.

The Garden

Genesis 2

In the east, God planted a beautiful garden in Eden. The garden was full of fruit-bearing trees and in the middle was the tree of life and the tree of the knowledge of good and evil. A river flowed from Eden to water the garden and then branched out in four different directions to flow through other lands.

God gave this plentiful garden to the first man, Adam, to enjoy and look after. As they walked together through the garden, God told him, "You may eat from every tree, except for one. If you eat from the tree of the knowledge of good and evil, then you shall die."

God did not want Adam to be alone but to have some help in the garden. God formed animals and brought them to him to give them names. But there were none among the animals that could be Adam's helper, so God made the first woman and brought her to Adam. Together they could talk and laugh and love, and plan and look after the garden with God.

The Tempting Fruit

Genesis 3

Of all the wild animals in the garden, the serpent was the craftiest. The creature was filled with the desire to spoil all the wondrous creation that God had made. The serpent met the woman and asked, "Did God say that you must not eat the fruit from any tree in the garden?"

The woman replied, "We may eat the fruit from any tree except from that one in the middle of the garden. God says if we touch it, we shall die."

The serpent moved closer and whispered, "You will not die if you eat that fruit, but you will be like God, knowing everything. That is why God has told you not to touch it."

The woman moved closer to the tree of the knowledge of good and evil. The fruit looked more appealing than that of every other tree. She imagined how lovely it would taste. She also thought how wonderful it would be to be wise like God and know everything, as the serpent had said. Reaching out, she picked one of the tempting fruits and bit into it. She passed it to Adam, who also took a bite.

But instead of feeling wise and clever, they felt afraid and ashamed. They knew that they had disobeyed God, who had lovingly created them and given them every good thing. They sewed some large leaves together to cover their bodies and hid among the trees from God.

The Separation

Genesis 3

As the evening breeze swept through the garden, God came to be with them. But the man and the woman stayed hidden. They used to love hearing God's call, but now they were fearful.

God called to them, "Where are you?"

Slowly the man and woman came out to meet God. The man replied, "I was afraid to see you because I was naked."

"Who told you that?" asked God. "Have you eaten from the tree of the knowledge of good and evil?"

Adam quickly said, "Yes, but it was not my fault. I was given the fruit to eat by the woman."

"But it was not my fault," the woman said. "The serpent tricked me into eating it."

The serpent was pleased with what it had done, spoiling what God had created.

God spoke to each of them. They had turned away and now life would be much harder for them. They would have to work on the land to produce plants to eat, and thorns and weeds would grow among them. There would now be hate and pain and death.

Finally, God said, "Because you have chosen to do want you wanted to do, you can no longer stay in the garden."

With great sadness, Adam and the woman, Eve, left the beautiful garden of Eden. Now, one of God's messengers with a sword of flame guarded the way to the tree of life.

The Great Flood

Genesis 4–7

Adam and Eve had two children, Cain and Abel. When the boys grew up, Abel looked after the sheep and Cain tilled the land to produce crops. Abel knew and loved God and offered the first of his new lambs, and God was pleased. Cain kept the best crops for himself and offered only the fruit of the ground to God, which God rejected. In a jealous and angry rage, Cain killed his brother. He left home to wander even further away from Eden. He and his wife had a child, who went on to have further children, who became fathers and mothers, too. Enoch built a city. Jabal was the ancestor of those who lived in tents and kept livestock. Tubal-Cain made all kinds of bronze and iron tools.

Meanwhile, Adam and Eve had another child, Seth. His descendants also became many people. Some loved God, but more and more went their own way. They fought as warriors and thought only of themselves. God saw what was happening and was greatly saddened. "I will blot out all people along with the animals that I have created, for I am sorry that I have made them."

However, there was one man named Noah who was faithful to God, along with his family. God spoke to him, saying, "I will be flooding the earth to destroy all living things. Make yourselves a huge ark of cypress wood. Cover it inside and out with tar and make a roof. On three decks, make rooms for you and your family and two of every kind of animal, male and female. Also take with you every kind of food that is eaten and store it well. This will be food for you all to eat during your time in the ark."

Noah did everything just as God instructed. When the ark was ready, the animals were taken inside. There was every kind of wild and tame animal, from the smallest to the largest; those that flew, leaped, and crawled. Finally, Noah, his wife, and his sons, Seth, Ham, and Japheth, and their wives also went into the ark. God closed the door, and the rain began.

The Rainbow Promise

Genesis 7–9

As the rain fell, flooding the earth, the ark was lifted by the water and floated on the surface. The flood continued for forty days and forty nights. The water rose so high that it covered the tallest mountains.

But God remembered Noah, his family, and the animals in the ark. After the rain, God sent a wind to blow over the earth, so that the water went down. There was so much water that this took time. Seven months passed, until finally the ark came to rest on the mountains of Ararat. Three months later, the tops of other mountains appeared. For those inside the ark, the waiting continued. After a further forty days, Noah sent out a raven, but it went to and fro, scavenging. Noah also sent out a dove to see if there were any signs of new life, but it returned to the ark as there was nowhere yet for it to rest. Seven days later, Noah released the dove again. To Noah's delight and joy, the dove returned with an olive leaf in its beak. He knew that the waters had subsided, and new life was springing up over the earth. After another seven days, Noah sent out the dove once again, and this time it did not return. He removed the roof of the ark, looked out, and saw the drying ground. Over the coming month, he watched as the earth dried completely.

Then God spoke to Noah: "It is time to leave the ark and begin again. Bring out your family and all the animals. The animals can again roam the earth and enjoy its goodness. Let life return and thrive."

The door of the ark opened, and the animals flew, leaped, and creeped out of the ark and onto land once more. With a thankful heart, Noah built an altar and made an offering to God. God blessed his family and a wonderful rainbow appeared through the clouds.

God said, "I am making a covenant with you and your descendants. I promise to never again send a flood to destroy all living things on earth. The rainbow is a sign of peace between us."

The Tower of Confusion

Genesis 10–11

THE FAMILIES DESCENDING from Noah's sons spread out across the land. They spoke one language, which unified them. However, this made them ambitious and they wanted to make themselves famous. They decided to build an impressive city that would be seen far and wide. The great city would reach as high as the heavens, for they saw themselves as powerful and important as God.

God saw them building the towering city and knew that their pride and ambition would only increase. Their schemes would become more dangerous and foolish. So God confused their language so that they could no longer understand each other. The people stopped building and scattered across the world. The place of the unfinished city was named Babel.

A Man Chosen

Genesis 12

ALTHOUGH PEOPLE WERE now scattered, God had a wonderful plan to choose a nation for a special purpose. This plan would begin with one man. God would share this plan with him and show him great love and blessings.

Many of the descendants of Noah's son Shem settled in the fertile plains of Mesopotamia. One family decided to travel from their home in the trading city of Ur to the land of Canaan, but they stopped at Haran and settled once again. A man named Abram was part of this family. He loved God and faithfully followed God's way. His wife was Sarai, and they shared a great sadness, for they were unable to have children. God chose Abram to fulfil his plan.

God spoke to him, saying, "Leave your country and your father's house and go to the land of Canaan. From you, I will make a great nation, and your name will become great."

Abram was seventy-five years old. He marvelled at God's words; with new hope, he followed God's call. He left the comfort of his home to live as a tent-dwelling nomad. Sarai and his nephew, Lot, went with him, along with the many servants and herdsmen of their household. Their sheep and goats were herded along, and donkeys carried all the baggage. Slowly, they wandered from one well or spring to the next, setting up their tents each evening. Every day they grew closer to the land of Canaan, as God had planned.

A Second Covenant

Genesis 12–15

When Abram arrived in Canaan, God spoke to him once more: "This is the land that I will be giving to your children." With continued hope, Abram explored the length of the land. He built altars to make offerings to God, and God blessed him, making him rich with plenty of sheep and goats. Lot too owned a great many sheep and goats, and the herdsmen of Abram and Lot began to argue at the wells and areas of freshest grass.

Abram said to Lot, "Families should not argue, so we must separate. Although I am older, I will let you choose which way you would like to go."

Lot chose to go east to settle in the lush green valley of the River Jordan, so Abram was left to go west to the bare, rocky hills. But Lot was soon caught up in trouble between warring city chiefs and taken hostage. Abram went to rescue him and set Lot free.

Despite Abram's fame, he did not want further riches. He and Sarai continued to long for children, but now they were getting too old.

One starry evening, God led Abram outside his tent and said, "Look up and count the stars, if you are able for there are so many of them. This will be the number of your descendants. I give to you this land."

Abram replied, "How am I to know?"

For the promise to be binding, God guided Abram to cut in two a young cow, and a young female and male goat, and also to lay down a turtle dove and a young pigeon. Abram fell into a deep, dark, and terrifying sleep. God showed him that his offspring would be strangers in a distant land and be slaves there for 400 years, but afterwards they would be released with great wealth.

In the night, God passed through the pieces with a smoking fire-pot and a flaming torch. "This is my covenant with you. To your descendants, I give this land from the river of Egypt to the great river of Mesopotamia."

Hagar's Child

Genesis 16

ABRAM HAD FAITH in God, but, as the years passed, still he and Sarai had no children. They wondered if another plan was needed to fulfil God's promise. In their household was an Egyptian slave girl named Hagar. At that time, the custom was to take another wife to solve the issue of being childless. Sarai offered Hagar to Abram to marry and bear a child.

When Hagar became pregnant, she began to boast and consider herself more important than Sarai. This upset and angered Sarai, and she complained to Abram. Abram allowed her to treat Hagar badly. In desperation, Hagar ran away into the dry, hot desert.

As Hagar was resting by a desert spring, a messenger from God appeared to her, asking, "Where have you come from?"

Hagar replied, "I am running away from my mistress, Sarai."

The messenger said, "Go back to her and do not boast. God has heard your cries and will look after you. You will bear a son, and name him Ishmael."

Hagar was amazed that God had seen her plight and would help her. "You are El Roi: the God who sees."

Hagar returned to Sarai and Ishmael was born, but he was not the son of Abram and Sarai that God had promised. Abram was now eighty-six years old.

The Laughing Son

Genesis 17–18; 21

Many more years passed. Abram was ninety-nine years old when once again God renewed his covenant with him. "I am God – walk before me and be blameless. You will no longer be named Abram, but your name shall be Abraham. You will be the ancestor of many nations, and kings will be your descendants. All the land of Canaan will be theirs for ever and I will be their God. Your wife will be named Sarah and I will bless her with a son."

Abraham laughed for he could not believe that he and Sarah, who was now ninety years old, were still able to have a child.

One day, as the midday sun beat down, Abraham was sitting at the entrance of his tent, and Sarah was keeping cool inside. Abraham looked up and saw three visitors standing near him. He ran to meet them, offering them water, food, and shade under the tree. Abraham and Sarah hurriedly prepared a good meal for their unexpected visitors. Bread was baked, a calf was killed and cooked, and Abraham set the meal before the guests with milk and cream.

As they ate, the guests spoke to Abraham. "Where is your wife?"

"She is inside the tent," replied Abraham.

One said, "I promise I will return within the year and your wife Sarah will have had a son."

Overhearing from inside the tent, Sarah laughed for she thought she was too old to now bear a child.

"Why did Sarah laugh?" said the guest. "Is anything too difficult for the Lord? I will do as I have promised."

Abraham and Sarah were shocked. They realized that their guests were not ordinary men but spoke the words of God.

Just as the visitor had said, Sarah bore a son. The son was named Isaac, meaning "he laughs" for God had brought laughter and joy to Sarah and Abraham.

The Test of Sacrifice

Genesis 22

Now that Isaac had been born, Sarah no longer wished for Hagar and Ishmael to live with them. Abraham was concerned, but God reassured him that nations would grow through both his children.

Abraham gave Hagar and her son some bread and water and sent them away to wander in the desert. When the food and water ran out and Hagar thought they would both die, God once again heard her cries.

"Do not be afraid," God said to her. "Ishmael will not die. I will make his descendants into a great nation." God opened her eyes and showed her a well nearby, so that she was able to give water to Ishmael. She knew that God was watching over them both.

Meanwhile, Isaac grew up loved greatly by his mother and father. Abraham knew that through Isaac, God's wonderful promise would be fulfilled. But one day, God called to Abraham, saying, "Take your only son, Isaac, whom you dearly love, to the far-off land of Moriah, and offer him as a sacrifice to me on the mountain."

All through his life Abraham had learned to trust and have faith in God so he did as God asked. Leaving early in the morning with his son and two servants, Abraham took a donkey loaded with the cut wood for burning. After three days, they arrived at the mountain. Abraham instructed the servants to stay with the donkey and walked on with Isaac, carrying the wood.

As they walked together, Isaac asked his father, "We have the wood for burning, but where is the lamb for the offering?"

"God will provide the lamb, my son," replied Abraham.

God showed Abraham the place where he was to build the altar. He piled the rocks and laid out the wood. Then, turning to his son, he tied his hands and feet, and with a heavy heart lifted him and laid him on top of the wood. Following God's instructions, Abraham took out his knife to kill his son.

Just at that moment, God spoke: "Abraham! Abraham! Do not strike the boy. Now I know that you love, respect, and glorify me above all else."

Trembling with relief, Abraham looked up and saw a ram caught in a thorny bush by its horns. He unbound Isaac, and taking the ram that God had provided, burned this as an offering instead of his son.

The Birthright

Genesis 24–25; 27

God continued to bless Abraham and his family. Isaac grew up and married Rebekah, the granddaughter of Abraham's brother. Although Isaac knew of God's promise to his father about having many descendants, he and Rebekah had no children for many years. After Abraham died, Isaac prayed to God to send them a child. Rebekah soon found that she was expecting two children, as she could sense them struggling together within her. At that time, the custom was that the eldest son inherited all the family rights and possessions. However, God told Rebekah that this time the younger son would become the head of the family. She pondered on this. When Rebekah gave birth, the first twin was a red-haired boy, and he was named Esau. Because he was gripping Esau's heel as he was born, the second twin boy, who had fair hair, was named Jacob.

As the boys grew up, Esau became a skilled hunter and worked in the fields, while Jacob lived a quieter life. Isaac loved Esau for he provided the meat to make delicious stews, but Rebekah loved Jacob most and remembered God's words.

One day, Esau returned from the fields and Jacob was cooking a delicious stew. Esau was very hungry and eager to eat some. Jacob saw his chance, saying, "I'll give you some stew if first you give me the rights of the firstborn son." Impatiently, Esau promised and gave away his birthright for the bowl of stew. He quickly forgot the matter.

As the years passed, Isaac became blind and frail. He knew it was time to pass on his blessing before he died. He summoned Esau and told him to hunt for a deer, prepare the stew for him, and then he would receive his father's blessing. Rebekah overheard Isaac and went to tell Jacob for she knew that he should receive the special blessing instead. She told Jacob to kill two young goats from the herd and she would prepare a fine stew. Jacob dressed in Esau's clothes and Rebekah wrapped the skins of the goats around Jacob's neck and arms. He would smell and feel like his brother.

Hoping the trick would work, Jacob carried the stew to Isaac.

"My father," Jacob said. "It is me, Esau, and I have done as you have told me."

Isaac was doubtful as he heard Jacob's voice, but he could smell Esau's clothes and feel his hairy skin. He ate the stew and then gave Jacob his blessing in God's name. Jacob would become the head of the whole family.

A Lesson Learned

Genesis 28–29

When Esau returned and learned of what had happened, he was enraged and vowed to kill Jacob. Rebekah knew that she had to protect Jacob, so she sent him away to live with her brother Laban.

One night as he journeyed, Jacob lay down to sleep, using a flat stone as a pillow. As he slept, he had a dream. He saw a shining ladder reaching from earth to heaven, and angels ascending and descending. In wonder, Jacob saw God standing beside him. God spoke, saying, "I am your God, the God of Abraham and of your father Isaac. I will give the land around you to you and your descendants. They will become a great nation and I will bless all people of the world through them. Know that I will be with you, wherever you go, and will bring you back to this land."

Jacob woke and in awe of God, praised him and set a stone to mark the place. He prayed, "If you are with me, then I will faithfully serve you all my life."

When Jacob came to his uncle's land, he saw some shepherds waiting for their flocks to drink from the well. A beautiful girl approached with her flock. The shepherds told Jacob that this was his uncle's daughter, Rachel. Jacob rolled the stone away from the well's mouth so that her flock could drink.

Jacob was welcomed by his uncle Laban and helped to look after his flocks. Laban offered him payment, but instead Jacob requested to marry Rachel if he worked without pay for seven years. The time passed quickly for Jacob loved spending time with Rachel.

When the seven years had passed, a great wedding feast was held. But it was evening, and Jacob could not see the face of his bride. When morning came, Jacob realized he had been married to Laban's eldest daughter, Leah. Jacob learned what it was like to be tricked.

A Return Home

Genesis 29–33

FOLLOWING JACOB'S WEDDING to Leah, Laban explained to him that it was custom for the eldest daughter to be married first. Jacob complained. Laban then promised that after a week, Jacob could marry Rachel as well but in return he would have to work a further seven years. He accepted.

As time passed, Jacob took two more wives and all bore him sons, except for Rachel. He loved her the most, which made Leah unhappy. But Rachel too was unhappy and very jealous of Leah and the other wives because of all the sons they had. There was Reuben, Simeon, Levi, and Judah; then Dan, Naphtali, Gad, and Asher; Issachar, and Zebulun, and a daughter named Dinah. Finally, after years of waiting, Rachel bore Jacob a son named Joseph.

Jacob's plan was now to return home, so he asked Laban. But his uncle persuaded him to stay as his flocks had become so large with Jacob looking after them. Jacob in return asked Laban if he could keep any black lambs and speckled goats in the flock. As there were not many, Laban agreed. As time passed, many more black and speckled ones were born, and God made Jacob very successful despite Laban trying to cheat him.

One night, God told Jacob to return to his home in Canaan so in the morning while Laban was away, he set out. With him went his wives, their children, and all his animals. When Laban discovered that they were gone, he sped after them.

In a dream, God had warned Laban to not say a word against Jacob. Jacob promised Laban that he would look after his family, and Laban was able to say goodbye to them.

As Jacob journeyed home, he was worried about how his brother Esau would receive him. He knew that God would keep him safe and prayed for his protection. That night a stranger appeared and wrestled with him through the night. At sunrise, the stranger touched Jacob's hip so that he could no longer fight. Jacob knew this stranger was no ordinary man and asked for his blessing.

"You shall no longer be named Jacob," said the stranger. "Your name is Israel, which means to strive and persevere. You have persevered in your struggles with God and with other people."

Jacob knew he had once again met with God.

As he drew closer to home, he picked his finest animals and sent them ahead as a gift for Esau. His brother came with 400 men. Bowing low, Jacob bravely approached him, taking courage from God's protection. Esau rushed toward him and hugged him, welcoming Jacob home.

Dreams of Greatness

Genesis 37

God continued to watch over the family of Israel as they settled in the land of Canaan. The quarrels continued between his wives and their children, but Israel was glad that he had a large family. Sadly, Rachel died giving birth to another son, Benjamin. Because of his love for Rachel, Israel treated Joseph as if he was his eldest son. He gave Joseph a long robe with elegant sleeves as a sign of his great love. Joseph also reported back to his father about how well his brothers looked after the sheep. This made the older brothers very angry and they refused to speak to him.

God had also given Joseph the gift of interpreting dreams, but at first he was not aware of this and wondered about the meaning of his strange dreams. He excitedly told his brothers about them, not realizing that this would anger them further.

"Listen to this dream," Joseph said. "We were binding together sheaves of corn in a field. Suddenly my sheaf rose and stood upright, and your sheaves gathered around it and bowed down."

"Do you think that you will reign over us?" they angrily asked.

Joseph told his father and brothers about another strange dream. "In this dream, the sun, moon, and eleven stars were bowing down to me."

Even his father was upset. "Do you really think that I, your mother, and your brothers will bow before you?" he scolded. But Israel did wonder if this dream was God's way of telling him that Joseph was chosen to be someone very special.

Taken to Egypt

Genesis 37

One day, Israel sent Joseph to find his brothers for they had been away a long time with the flocks. After a search, eventually Joseph found his brothers, but as he approached, they recognized him by his long robe and planned to kill him. The eldest, Reuben, stopped his brothers and said, "Shed no blood. Just throw him into a dried-up well and leave him here in the desert." He hoped to rescue him once his other brothers had left.

When Joseph came near, the brothers stripped off his long robe and threw him into the well. As they ate nearby, a caravan of traders passed. The long line of camels carried spices, balm, and myrrh to trade in Egypt. The brothers decided to make some money and get rid of Joseph at the same time. They drew Joseph out of the well and sold him to the traders for twenty pieces of silver.

Reuben was horrified by what his brothers had done. They took Joseph's robe and dipped it into goat's blood and went to their father.

"We have found your son's robe," they lied.

In horror, Israel saw that it was Joseph's and believed that he had been devoured by a wild animal. He tore his clothes in grief and mourned the loss of his son for many days.

Meanwhile, Joseph had been sold into the household of Potiphar, the captain of the pharaoh's guard in Egypt.

Imprisoned

Genesis 39–40

God was with Joseph, and he worked hard in the house of Potiphar. Potiphar noticed that Joseph was successful in whatever he did and soon gave him responsibility over his whole household. But this was not to last, for Potiphar's wife had taken a liking to Joseph and wanted him to lie with her. He refused time and time again. One day she caught hold of his clothes, and he fled, leaving the piece of clothing in her hands. Out of spite, she told lies about Joseph to Potiphar, pretending that he had done wrong. Potiphar was enraged that the man he trusted had betrayed him and he threw Joseph into prison.

All seemed hopeless, but Joseph remained faithful to God, and God was with him. The chief jailer found that Joseph was helpful and trustworthy, and put him in charge of the care of the other prisoners. Whatever Joseph did was done well.

A while later, the pharaoh was angry with both his cupbearer, who poured his wine, and his chief baker. They joined Joseph in prison, and he looked after them. One night they both had dreams, and in the morning, Joseph found them very troubled. Concerned, Joseph asked them why they were miserable, and they told him about their dreams.

The cupbearer described his dream. "In my dream there was a vine with three branches. It budded, blossomed, and then clusters of

grapes ripened. I took the grapes, pressed them into the pharaoh's cup, and gave the cup to the pharaoh."

Joseph interpreted the dream. "In three days, Pharaoh will restore you to his household as cupbearer once again. Please remember me and ask the pharaoh to release me for I have done nothing wrong."

Hopeful that his dream would be favourable too, the chief baker told Joseph, "I dreamed that there were three baskets on my head. In the top basket, there were all sorts of delicious pastries for the pharaoh, but the birds were pecking at the food."

Joseph told him, "Within three days, the pharaoh will put you to death."

The interpretations were correct, and in three days the chief baker was hanged. The cupbearer returned to pouring the pharaoh's wine, but he forgot about Joseph.

Pharaoh's Dreams

Genesis 41

ALTHOUGH JOSEPH REMAINED in prison, God had not forgotten him and was preparing him for greatness. Two years passed, and then one night the pharaoh had a troubling dream. He was standing by the River Nile, and out of the water came seven healthy-looking cows that grazed in the reeds. Then seven thin cows came out of the Nile and ate the healthy cows. The pharaoh awoke abruptly. Falling asleep once again, he had a second dream. There were seven ears of grain, plump and healthy growing on one stalk. Then seven other ears of grain, thin and diseased, grew up after them and swallowed the healthy grain. Once again, the pharaoh awoke, very troubled. He summoned all his wise men, but no one could explain his dreams. As he was pouring the pharaoh's wine, the cupbearer remembered

Joseph and told the pharaoh about how Joseph had correctly interpreted his and the baker's dreams.

The pharaoh summoned Joseph from prison. Hastily, Joseph was washed, shaved, dressed in clean clothes, and brought before the pharaoh.

"I have heard that you can interpret dreams," said the pharaoh.

"It is not I, but my God who works through me," replied Joseph.

The pharaoh told him his dreams, and then Joseph explained them. "The dreams mean the same thing. The seven healthy cows and the seven healthy ears of grain mean that there will be seven years of good harvest. The seven thin cows and the seven diseased ears of grain mean that there will then follow seven years of famine. Therefore, appoint an overseer who stores grain during the good years so that there will be enough to survive the seven years of famine."

Impressed with the wisdom of Joseph, the pharaoh appointed him to be in charge of storing the grain. The pharaoh gave Joseph fine clothes, a gold chain, his signet ring, and a chariot.

"Only I will be greater than you," said the pharaoh. "Everyone else will bow before you."

The Famine

Genesis 41–42

As a slave and even in prison, Joseph had learned to trust God and do his work well. He continued to do the same as he set about his new work, storing grain in newly built storehouses in every city in Egypt during the seven years of plenty. Then came the famine. As governor of the land, Joseph made sure that the grain was fairly shared out. Soon, people from nearby countries journeyed to Egypt to ask for grain to take home to their own lands.

In the land of Canaan, Israel and his sons were hungry, too. Israel sent out ten of his sons to buy grain from Egypt; only Benjamin stayed behind with his father. They came before Joseph and bowed before him, not recognizing him as their brother, for he was dressed as a powerful Egyptian. Joseph knew who they were and wondered if they were sorry for what they had done. He decided to test them. He accused them of being spies, but they denied it and told him about themselves.

"We have just come to buy food," the brothers said. "We are twelve brothers. One is dead and the youngest has stayed at home with our father."

Joseph ordered that one brother, Simeon, would stay in prison while the others returned home with grain. To prove their story, Joseph told them that the next time they came, they must bring the youngest brother. When the brothers returned home, they were dismayed to discover that their bags of money were lying on top of the grain.

"We will be accused of being thieves as well as spies," they told their father. They did not know that Joseph had instructed his servants to do this to find out if his brothers still thought only of themselves.

A Family Reunion

Genesis 43–46

As the grain ran out, Israel once again had to send his sons to Egypt for more.

"We must go with Benjamin," said Judah to his father. "I promise on my life to take care of him."

Reluctantly Israel agreed. "Take double the money, and may God be with you."

To their amazement, Joseph gave them a fine welcome when he saw his brothers and Benjamin with them. He released Simeon and invited them to dinner, seating them in the order of their ages.

As they started on their return home with sacks full of grain, the brothers thought all was well. But then Joseph's steward rode up and stopped them and accused them of stealing a silver cup.

The brothers denied this, saying, "If any one of us has the cup, you can put him to death and keep the rest of us as slaves."

The sacks were opened. The last one was Benjamin's and nestled inside was the glimmering silver cup. Horrified, the brothers returned to Joseph's house. They did not know that Joseph had done this as part of his plan.

In front of Joseph, Judah stepped forward and humbly offered his own life instead of Benjamin's. "If Benjamin remains here, my father will die of grief," he pleaded.

Joseph knew that his brothers were very different now and no longer could he keep his identity from them. Weeping, he ordered his servants to leave the room, and then he said to his brothers, "I am your brother Joseph, whom you sold into slavery. God has always been with me. Go and bring my father and all your households to Egypt to live with me."

The brothers were amazed and filled with wonder and joy, and the whole household of Israel moved to Egypt. Joseph was once more reunited with his father, Israel.

A Baby Saved

Exodus 1–2

THE HOUSEHOLD OF Israel settled well in Egypt. They had many children, who continued to flourish. The Israelites soon became a great number. The pharaoh who knew Joseph died and other pharaohs came to the throne who did not know what Joseph had done for Egypt. They viewed the Israelites as foreigners and hated them living in Egypt.

One new pharaoh was fearful and saw the great number of Israelites as a threat to his power. He decided to make them weak by forcing them to work as slaves, building great new cities. But the more the pharaoh ill-treated them, the more the people of Israel grew in number. Ruthlessly, the pharaoh decided to make a new law, commanding, "Every boy that is born to the Israelites is to be drowned in the River Nile."

God had not deserted the descendants of Israel and set in place a rescue plan. One Israelite woman named Jochebed tried to hide away her newborn son, but after three months she knew that she could hide him no longer as his cries grew louder. She took a basket made of papyrus reeds and covered it with tar so that water would not seep into it. She gently laid her sleeping baby in the basket and went down to the Nile. She took her daughter Miriam along with her.

Placing the basket in among the reeds, Jochebed asked Miriam, "Watch over your baby brother a short distance away to see what happens to him."

A while later the pharaoh's daughter came down to bathe in the river. She saw the basket and heard the baby crying. Her maid brought the basket to her. The princess said, "Poor thing! He must be an Israelite baby."

Thinking swiftly, Miriam approached the princess. Bravely she asked, "Shall I fetch an Israelite lady to nurse the child for you?"

The princess agreed, and Miriam hurriedly went to fetch her mother. The princess said to Jochebed, "Take this baby and I will pay you to nurse him for me. When he is older, bring him to the palace so that he can be my son. I drew him out of the water, so I shall name him Moses."

Joyously, Jochebed and Miriam took Moses home knowing that he was now safe.

The Burning Bush

Exodus 3–4

God continued to hear the cries of suffering of the Israelites, and remembered the covenants with Abraham, Isaac, and Jacob. Moses grew up in the palace as an Egyptian prince, but he knew that he was an Israelite. One day he saw an Egyptian beating a slave and was so angry that he struck the Egyptian, killing him. When Moses realized that his deed was known, he fled from the palace and ran far away to the land of Midian.

Moses became a hard-working humble shepherd, married, and had a son. The pharaoh died but the new one continued to treat the Israelites cruelly. God noticed this.

One day, Moses was tending his father-in-law's flock on the mountain of Horeb. Suddenly a bush before him was blazing brightly but not being burned.

God's voice came from the bush, calling, "Moses! Moses!"

"Here I am," replied Moses.

"Take off your sandals," God said, "for you stand on holy ground."

Moses removed his sandals from his feet and covered his face for he knew he was in the presence of God.

"I am the God of your father," God said. "I have heard the cries of my people in Egypt, and I am going to rescue them. I will send you to lead them out and into the land that I promised to give to the descendants of Abraham. I will be with you."

Moses did not wish to be God's leader. He did not want to go back to Egypt. He made excuses, but for each one God had an answer.

"Suppose the Israelites do not believe that you have sent me," Moses feared.

"Throw your staff onto the ground," God instructed. As Moses did this, the staff turned into a snake. He leaped back in alarm, but God then said, "Reach out your hand and seize its tail." As Moses did this, the snake became a staff in his hand once more.

"The Israelites will know that I have appeared to you and am with you. The Egyptians will know that I am more powerful than the gods they worship," reassured God.

Eventually Moses had no further excuses. His brother Aaron would help him and be the spokesperson, and he was to show the power of God to the pharaoh.

The Plagues

Exodus 4–10

As Moses returned with his wife and child to Egypt, Aaron came out to meet him. Moses told him all that God had instructed. They met first with the Israelite leaders, and they praised God that they were to be rescued.

Next, Moses and Aaron went to see the pharaoh, and said, "The God of Israel says, 'Let my people go free.'"

But the pharaoh replied, "Who is this God? I will not do this."

He told his servants to work the slaves harder. Now they would have to cut the straw from the fields themselves to make the bricks. Life was worse than ever for the Israelites. They were angry with Moses and Aaron.

Moses turned to God, saying, "Why did you ever send me?"

God replied, "Now you will all see my power. The pharaoh will let my people go."

Moses warned the pharaoh once more that terrifying disasters would happen, but the pharaoh did not listen. Moses raised his stick over the River Nile and God turned the water into blood, so that everything in the water died and rotted. Seven days later, the pharaoh again refused, so God sent a plague of frogs, then gnats, and then flies. The animals of the Egyptians then died, and the people were covered in painful boils, but despite being asked after each disaster, still the pharaoh would not let the Israelites go. God sent thunder and hail, ruining the crops, and then a plague of locusts that consumed all the remaining food. Then for three days, darkness fell across all of Egypt. God saw that the pharaoh did not listen and was not changing his mind.

Exodus

Exodus 11–14

Finally, God told Moses, "I will bring one more terrible disaster, the death of the firstborn son of every family. Then the pharaoh will let my people go. Tell the Israelites to stay safe by killing an unblemished lamb for each household and daub its blood over the door and the doorposts of their houses. Then roast the lamb for a special dinner and eat it all with bitter herbs and unleavened bread, for there is no time for it to rise. When it gets dark, the whole family must stay inside."

The Israelites prepared as Moses told them for the night of the Passover.

At midnight, a loud and terrible wail of grief came from the homes of the Egyptians. The pharaoh summoned Moses and Aaron, and said, "Rise up and leave Egypt. Take everything you own and be gone."

The Israelite families gathered their belongings and herded their animals. The Egyptians had given them gold and silver so that they would not return.

Ahead of them, God went as a pillar of cloud to offer shade by day, and as a pillar of fire to show the way at night. The Israelites kept journeying through the wilderness toward the Red Sea.

Meanwhile in Egypt, the pharaoh changed his mind for now he

no longer had the Israelites as slaves. He and his army pursued the Israelites in chariots, so they gained on them swiftly.

As the pharaoh drew near to the Red Sea, the Israelites looked in horror at the approaching army and cried out to God. Moses told them to not be afraid for God would protect them. The pillar of cloud moved behind the Israelites to prevent the Egyptians coming closer.

God then spoke to Moses, saying, "Stretch out your hand over the sea."

As Moses did this, the water divided, leaving a way through on dry ground. The Israelites walked across, but the Egyptians chased after them. Seeing this, God caused their chariot wheels to become clogged and the Egyptians were thrown into confusion.

God then said to Moses, "Stretch out your hand so that the water will flow once more."

As the sea returned to its normal depth, the Egyptian army was washed away. The Israelites saw and believed in the power of God and celebrated the wondrous rescue.

The Ten Commandments

Exodus 16–32

As the Israelites wandered on through the hot dry desert, they began to complain about being hungry and thirsty. God provided for them, sending quails for them to eat in the evening, and in the morning the people gathered a fine, flaky, wafer-like meal in the dew, which they called manna. To drink, God told Moses to strike a rock, and water gushed from it.

After many weeks of journeying, the people arrived at the base of a mountain in the Sinai desert. God called to Moses from the mountain, saying, "Tell the Israelites that I have brought them out of Egypt under my care and protection as on eagles' wings. If they love and obey me, following what is good and right to do, then they will be my chosen nation. I will speak to you, Moses, in front of them all so that they know you are my chosen leader."

Three days later, the people gathered around the mountain. Thunder and lightning flashed around the mountain, which was wrapped in smoke. A loud, long blast of a trumpet resounded through the cloud, and the people trembled with fear.

God spoke and all heard. "I am the Lord your God; you shall not worship other gods.

"Do not make images to worship.

"Do not misuse my name.

"Keep the sabbath day holy, set aside especially for God.

"Respect your parents.

"Do not murder.

"Do not commit adultery.

"Do not steal.

"Do not tell lies about others.

"Do not want something that belongs to another."

The people were so afraid to hear God's voice through the thunder and lightning that they begged Moses to listen to God and then report back to them about what God was saying. Moses went into the cloud and was gone for forty days and forty nights. God told Moses the laws and instructions about how the Israelites would live as a special nation of God, different to how other nations lived and worshipped. God spoke about the festivals to hold through the year, the role and clothing of the priests, and exactly how to build a tabernacle, a special tent, which was to be the meeting place of God's presence among the people. Written with the finger of God, the ten commandments were carved into two stone tablets, which Moses carried down from the mountain.

Meanwhile, the people tired of waiting for Moses. They looked to Aaron and told him to make a god who would lead them. The people gave him all their gold trinkets, and Aaron melted them down and remoulded them into a golden calf.

"Tomorrow, we shall have a festival," Aaron proclaimed, and the people were delighted. They feasted and drank and behaved wildly.

The Tabernacle

Exodus 32–40

God knew what was happening and was angered that the people had turned away so quickly. Moses begged God to remember the promises to Abraham, Isaac, and Jacob, and went down the mountain to find out what had angered God. When Moses saw how the people were behaving, he was horrified and threw down the stone tablets at the foot of the mountain. He burned the calf in the fire, so it melted once more, ground the gold into powder to mix with water, and made the Israelites drink it.

The next day, the people were ashamed about what they had done. Moses returned to ask God to forgive the people. He offered to take the blame, but God said that whoever had done wrong must be sorry. God remade the two stone tablets for Moses to take back to the people and promised once again to still be with them.

As Moses came down from Mount Sinai, the skin of his face shone for he had been in God's presence. The people offered their fine possessions to make the tabernacle and a gold-covered ark for storing the stone tablets. The lid of the ark was a mercy seat with two figures with outspread wings covering the tablets, as God would cover and forgive the people's wrongdoings.

Moses placed the ark inside the tabernacle and set up a curtain in front as a screen. Before the curtain, Moses placed a golden altar with the offering of fragrant incense. On the north side was a gold-covered table with some bread for the Lord, and on the south side was the golden lampstand with seven lamps. A screen was set up for the entrance and before this was put the altar of burned-offering to request forgiveness and the grain-offering at special times to say thank you. A bronze basin with water for washing hands and feet was also placed at the entrance for the priests to use before they entered. A courtyard was set up around all of this and a screen put up at the gate. Everything could be carried when the Israelites journeyed.

When God's presence filled the tabernacle, a dazzling cloud covered the tent. Whenever the cloud lifted, the Israelites would set out on the next stage of their journey toward the Promised Land.

The Spies

Numbers 13–14

As the Israelites approached the Promised Land, God told Moses to send out twelve men, one from each of the tribes of Israel, to spy out the land. The tribes formed from the households of the twelve sons of Israel.

The spies returned carrying grapes, figs, and pomegranates, reporting, "The land flows with milk and honey, and this is its fruit. But the people who live there are strong, and the towns are well fortified. They are like giants while we seem like grasshoppers."

The Israelites were fearful and complained, "Why did God bring us here to die? It would be better if we returned to Egypt."

Joshua and Caleb, who had been two of the twelve spies, said, "Do not fear the people. God will help us."

But the Israelites did not listen to them. Then God's cloud appeared over the tabernacle, and God spoke to Moses. "How long will these people refuse to believe and trust me, despite everything that I have done for them? None of those who came out of Egypt will enter this land but will wander in the wilderness, except for Joshua and Caleb. They will lead the next generation into this land after forty years."

So the people turned back into the dry, dusty desert.

Balaam's Donkey

Numbers 22–24

FORTY YEARS PASSED and the Israelites moved closer to the Promised Land once again, reaching the banks of the River Jordan. There were so many of them that they were now greatly feared by those living in the surrounding area. The Israelites camped in the land of Moab. The king of Moab, Balak, wanted to be rid of them so he sent messengers to summon a wise man named Balaam.

"Come now to curse these people, who have settled next to me," requested the king. The messengers offered money to Balaam to do this.

That night God spoke to Balaam, saying, "Do not go, for you shall not curse the people that I bless."

Balaam refused to go to Moab. Hearing this, King Balak sent more riches of gold and silver to persuade him. So Balaam saddled his donkey and journeyed back with the messengers, thinking only of the money.

As they rode, the donkey suddenly turned off the road and into a field. In the road was a messenger sent by God, standing with a drawn sword. Balaam could not see this and beat the donkey, turning it back onto the road.

Then as they were going along a narrow path with a wall on either side, God's messenger appeared again. The donkey tried to squeeze past, crushing Balaam's foot against the wall. Balaam beat the donkey again.

A third time, God's messenger barred the way. The donkey, unable to pass, lay down. Balaam struck the donkey again. Suddenly, to his amazement, the donkey spoke. "Why are you beating me? Have I ever behaved like this before?"

Then God opened Balaam's eyes to see his messenger with the drawn sword ahead of them.

"Why have you beaten your donkey?" God's messenger said. "She has saved your life three times. Go on, but speak only what I tell you to say."

When Balaam reached King Barak, he prepared carefully to curse the Israelites. But Balaam could only say what God told him and so he could not curse them. Instead, he blessed them. He tried four times, but each time only blessings and predictions of the Israelites' strength and success were uttered.

Entering the Promised Land

Deuteronomy 31; Joshua 1–4

THE TIME WAS near for the Israelites to enter the Promised Land. At the end of his life, Moses led Joshua into the tabernacle to be in God's presence.

God spoke to Joshua, saying, "Be strong and courageous for you will lead the Israelites into the land that I promised them. I will be with you."

To enter the land, the Israelites not only had to cross the fast-flowing River Jordan but also defeat the great walled city of Jericho. So Joshua secretly sent two spies to investigate the city. The king of Jericho found out and sent soldiers to find them. A brave woman named Rahab hid the spies in her house and directed the soldiers to search elsewhere.

Rahab told the spies, "We know that God has given you the land and we all fear you. Protect my family when you come into the city just as I have protected you."

The spies told her to tie a crimson cord in the window and she and her family would be protected. Rahab helped the spies escape the city, letting them down by a rope through the window of her house, which was in the city wall.

Joshua prepared the Israelites to cross the fast-flowing river, trusting God's orders: "Priests carrying the ark of the Lord's covenant will lead you into the river. Then you must all follow."

As the priests carrying the precious ark stepped into the river, the water's flow began to slow until it stopped completely. The ground was dry beneath their feet. They moved to the middle of the Jordan and stood there as all the Israelites crossed over.

Joshua then sent twelve men, one from every tribe of Israel, to pick up a stone each from where the priests stood, and said, "When your children ask in time to come, 'What do those stones mean to you?' then you shall tell them how the waters of the Jordan were stopped in front of the ark of the Lord. These stones will be a memorial for ever."

The Fall of Jericho

Joshua 5–24

NEWS SPREAD THAT God had dried up the Jordan so that the Israelites could cross. The kings of the Amorites to the west and those of Canaan were disheartened. The gates of Jericho were closed, and no one came in or out. Joshua continued to be guided by God and received instructions about how the city would be taken.

Early one morning, seven priests each with a trumpet of ram horn went before those carrying the ark of the Lord's covenant. All the warriors marched in front and behind them. The procession went around the walls once, with the priests blowing their trumpets continually. No one spoke. They did the same thing for six days.

On the seventh day, they marched in the same way, but this time went around the walls seven times. The priests then blew a long, loud blast and the people shouted with all their might, making a great noise. The walls of the city shook, weakened by the vibrations, and crumbled. The Israelites took the city, sparing Rahab and her family, who had saved the spies.

This was the first of many cities taken by the Israelites. When Joshua and his leaders listened to God, their attacks were successful. After many campaigns, they had taken land to the north and to the south. Some parts of the land of Canaan were rich and fertile and other parts were stony and poor. God chose Joshua with a priest and some leaders to share out the country among the twelve tribes. There were the tribes of Reuben, Simeon, and Judah; Issachar, Zebulun, Benjamin, and Dan; Naphtali, Gad, and Asher. The tribes of Manasseh and Ephraim were named after Joseph's two sons. The tribe of Levi was not given any land to look after for their special role was to be God's priests. Every other tribe was to share a part of their supplies with them.

Once the land had been allocated, Joshua gathered the tribes, and once again they renewed their covenant with God.

“As promised, God has given us plentiful land that we have not farmed, and cities that we did not build. God has done mighty and wondrous things and protected us. Will you serve God?” Joshua asked them.

The people agreed and promised not to follow other gods.

The Time of the Judges

Judges 1–8

AFTER THE DEATH of Joshua, the Israelites had no leader and the next generations began to do things their own way. They married into the families of the people of Canaan and took on their worship of many gods. This weakened the tribes and strengthened the Canaanites, who fought against them and made them suffer by charging heavy taxes. The people on their borders, such as the Moabites, the Ammonites, and the Philistines, attacked them and plundered their land.

When the Israelites became completely desperate, they remembered God and cried out for help. God remembered them and sent leaders, who helped to free them from their enemies. These leaders listened to God, advising and guiding the people wisely, and were known as the judges.

One of these times was when the Midianites caused great suffering in Israel. Whenever the Israelites tried to crow crops, the Midianites rode across on their camels to raid the land, taking the produce, and seizing their animals. Israel was weak, poor, and defenceless.

A messenger sent from God appeared to a warrior named Gideon, who was hiding wheat in the wine press.

"God is with you," said the messenger.

"Why then is all this happening to us?" replied Gideon. "Where are all God's wondrous deeds that our ancestors told us about? God has cast us off!"

"God is sending you to save Israel from suffering at the hand of the Midianites," said the messenger.

Gideon did not believe this for he was from the weakest tribe of all Israel.

"If I am the one, show me a sign," Gideon said.

He prepared some meat, a broth, and some unrisen cakes and put them on a rock before God's messenger. The messenger touched them with a staff and fire sprang up, consuming them.

Gideon gathered men from the tribes of Israel to fight the Midianites, but he still needed convincing that they would be successful.

He laid some wool on the ground and said to God, "In the morning if there is dew on the fleece but the ground is dry, I shall know."

The next morning, Gideon was able to squeeze out a bowlful of water from the fleece and yet the ground was dry.

"Please don't be angry," Gideon said, "but can I have one more sign? This time if the fleece is dry and the ground is covered in dew, I shall know."

Again, God gave him the proof. So, Gideon led the gathered Israelite army and they camped across the valley from the Midianite camp.

God spoke to Gideon, saying, "You have too many men. I want to show you all that I have the power to free you and defeat your enemies. Tell anyone who is afraid to go home."

Some 22,000 went home, leaving 10,000 men in the camp.

God told Gideon, "There are still too many. Take them down to the river and separate those who lap the water with their tongues, drinking like dogs, and those who kneel down to drink."

Some 300 men lapped like dogs, bringing the water to their mouths. God told Gideon to send everyone else home and gave him instructions.

That night, Gideon divided the 300 men into three groups and gave each of them trumpets to blow and empty jars with torches inside. They took their position around the Midianites' camp. All together they blew the trumpets, and smashed the jars, causing a dazzling light. They cried out, "A sword for God and for Gideon!" The terrifying noise threw the Midianites into confusion and they began to fight each other, before fleeing. Gideon's army pursued them beyond the River Jordan.

Ruth, the Faithful Daughter-in-Law

Ruth 1–4

DURING THE TIME of the judges, there was a famine in the land. The harvest was poor and there was not enough food. Elimelek, who lived in the town of Bethlehem in Judah, moved with his wife Naomi and their two sons to the country of Moab. Sadly, Elimelek died. His two sons married Moabite women, one named Orpah and the other Ruth. About ten years later both Naomi's sons died, leaving her in a foreign land without a family to support her. Orpah and Ruth were kind and comforted her, but life was very tough for women without husbands and sons to look after them.

The famine had now passed in the land of Judah, so Naomi decided to return there. Orpah and Ruth set out with her, but Naomi told them to return to their own families for she could not offer them security and happiness. Weeping and with great reluctance, Orpah went back to her people, but Ruth was determined to go with Naomi.

"Do not press me to leave you, or to turn back," begged Ruth. "Where you go, I will go; where you shelter, I will shelter; your people shall become my people and your God shall become my God. Nothing will make me part from you, except death."

So Naomi and Ruth went on until they came to Bethlehem. They arrived at the time of the barley harvest. Although widows could not earn money, God had given the Israelites special laws to support those in need. The poor and hungry could pick up any grain stalks left behind by the reapers as they gathered the harvest. Eager to help Naomi, Ruth went to glean the grain stalks from a field belonging to a rich farmer named Boaz. Unknown to her, Boaz was related to Naomi's husband.

Later that day, Boaz came to oversee the reapers in the field and eat with them. He noticed Ruth and asked who she was. Hearing that she had returned with Naomi from Moab, he showed her great generosity.

"Follow close behind my reapers," Boaz told her. "If you are thirsty, drink from the water that my men have drawn. May the God of Israel reward you for the kindness that you have shown Naomi. Come and eat with my reapers."

Boaz also told his reapers to drop some barley stalks on purpose so that Ruth would have extra to take home.

When Naomi heard about Boaz, she encouraged Ruth to continue gleaning in his fields, but her thoughts turned to what would happen once the harvest was over. It was custom that a supper was held at the end of the gathering of the harvest. Naomi told Ruth to meet Boaz alone after the supper and ask for his care and protection for they were members of his family. Bravely, Ruth did exactly as Naomi told her. Boaz was delighted that Ruth had come to him for help, as he very much wanted to marry her.

"Do not be afraid," said Boaz. "I will do all that you ask, but there is a relative that is closer to Elimelek than I am. If he does not want to look after you then I shall."

Boaz sent her home with a generous measure of barley. He then met the relative and asked him if he wanted to help Naomi and Ruth. This meant buying the land that once belonged to Elimelek and marrying Ruth. The relative said he was unable to do this, so Boaz gladly bought the land and married Ruth.

Naomi was delighted and knew they had all been wonderfully blessed by God. She was even more overjoyed when Ruth and Boaz had a son named Obed, who was to become the father of Jesse. Their descendants would fulfil God's wonderful plan of promised hope.

Samuel, Born to Serve

1 Samuel 1–2

When the Israelites settled in Canaan, the tabernacle was set up in a place called Shiloh. The people would visit to bring offerings to give thanks and worship God. One of the priests was an old man named Eli.

One year, Eli overheard a woman praying. Her name was Hannah and although she had been married for many years, she had no children. She wept as she prayed silently. "O God, remember me, and give me a child. I will give him back to serve you all his life."

As only her lips were moving, Eli at first thought she was drunk and went to talk to her. When he heard of her sadness, he comforted her, saying, "Go in peace. May God answer your prayer."

Hannah's prayer was answered, and she had a son, whom she named Samuel. She did not forget her promise to God. When Samuel was old enough to dress and feed himself, she took him to Shiloh and asked Eli to look after him. Before she left, Hannah praised and gave thanks to God.

Each year, Hannah returned to visit Samuel, taking with her a new robe for him. God blessed her with more children, but she never forgot Samuel.

A Prophetic Calling

1 Samuel 3–6

SAMUEL WAS GUIDED by Eli as he grew and was loved by God and the people. Eli began to lose his sight, so Samuel helped him in the tabernacle. At night, when Eli slept in his own room, Samuel laid down in the tabernacle, making sure the lamp stayed lit before the ark of the Lord's covenant.

One night, Samuel heard a voice calling his name. Thinking it was Eli calling, Samuel hurried to him, saying, "Here I am."

But Eli replied, "I did not call. Lie down again."

Samuel lay down, but the voice called his name again. Samuel rushed to Eli, but Eli denied it was him and sent him back. The third time, Eli realized that God was calling Samuel so he told Samuel, "If you are called again, say, 'Speak, Lord, for your servant is listening.'"

As Samuel lay down, once more God called him: "Samuel! Samuel!"

Samuel replied, "Speak, Lord, for your servant is listening."

Then God told Samuel some shocking news. Eli had two sons who were not good. They were priests but they took from the offerings of the people and did not respect God. They behaved badly and disregarded God's Law. God would not allow them to be priests any longer.

Samuel lay awake until morning, afraid about how he would tell Eli this news. As usual he opened the doors to the tabernacle, and he could not avoid Eli.

Eli asked him, "What did God tell you? Do not hide anything from me."

So Samuel told him everything, and Eli accepted what God was to do.

A while later, the Philistines prepared to attack the Israelites. Eli's sons were with the ark of the Lord's covenant, which had been taken to the Israelites' camp. During the battle, Eli's sons were killed, and the ark captured by the Philistines. When Eli heard the news, he fell backwards in shock, broke his neck, and died.

The Philistines were at first delighted that they had captured the ark, but then misfortune fell on them wherever it was kept. They began to fear the God of Israel, so they put the ark with some peace offerings on a cart pulled by two cows. Without anyone guiding them, the cows pulled the cart into Israel and the ark was returned safely.

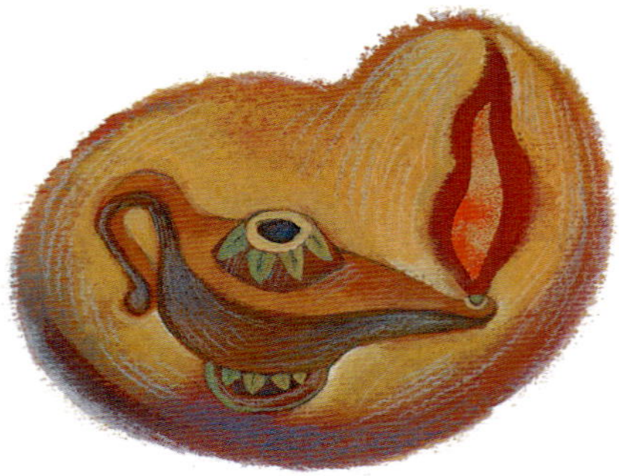

Israel's First King

1 Samuel 8–15

As Samuel grew up, God often appeared to him, giving him messages for the people of Israel. The Israelites trusted Samuel as a prophet. He guided them to turn away from worshipping their foreign gods and follow only God, who would protect them from their enemies, such as the Philistines and Ammonites.

Samuel became old and the elders of Israel were concerned that they had no leader.

They asked Samuel, "Appoint a king to govern us, like other nations have."

Samuel was displeased and God was angered, saying, "The people have rejected me from being their true king. Warn them and tell them the ways of kings."

So Samuel told the people that a king would send their sons into battle and tell them what to do. A king would keep the best for himself and take a tenth of their possessions.

Despite Samuel's warning, the people refused to listen. Samuel prayed, and God spoke: "Let them have their king. I shall send a man from the land of Benjamin and you shall anoint him. He shall save my people from their enemies."

A tall man named Saul was chosen by Samuel to be king. He was a farmer, but Samuel guided him in his duties. Israel's kings were to be different for they were to be guided by God, and not just do as they wanted. Although reluctant at first, Saul led the Israelites against the attacking Ammonite army with God's help. The Israelites were successful, and the people rejoiced that Saul was their king.

Saul became a soldier–king and led the Israelite army whenever countries on their borders attacked, especially the Philistines. Saul's son Jonathan also showed bravery in battle. But ahead of one battle, Saul became impatient waiting for Samuel to arrive and make an offering to God. Thinking he had the right as a powerful king, Saul prepared the offering himself. As he was finishing, Samuel arrived.

"You have acted foolishly," Samuel told him. "If you had followed God's commands, you and your descendants would have ruled over Israel for ever."

Overwhelmed by his power and influence, Saul began to do more things his own way, ignoring what Samuel told him were God's wishes. Samuel was disappointed and deeply saddened by Saul's actions, so God guided Samuel to anoint another.

The Shepherd Boy

1 Samuel 16

In Bethlehem, there was a man named Jesse, son of Obed and grandson of Ruth and Boaz. Guided by God, Samuel went to Bethlehem and held a feast, inviting Jesse and all his family. At the celebration, Samuel looked at Jesse's eldest son, who was handsome and tall, and thought surely this was the man that the Lord had chosen to be the next king.

But God said to Samuel, "Do not look on his outward appearance; I look at a person's thoughts and feelings. This man is not the one I have chosen."

In order of age, Samuel was introduced to seven of Jesse's sons, but God had not chosen any of them.

Samuel asked Jesse, "Are all your sons here?"

Jesse replied, "My youngest son is looking after the sheep."

Samuel insisted that he should come, for the feast could not begin without him. Quickly, someone fetched David from the fields. He arrived, looking tanned and healthy from an outdoor life.

"This is the one I have chosen," God guided Samuel. "Anoint him."

To David's amazement and in front of his brothers, Samuel took out a horn filled with oil. He sprinkled some drops on David's head, telling him God's message that one day he would be king. The spirit of God came upon David.

Slaying a Giant

1 Samuel 17

Meanwhile, Saul became disheartened without God's guidance. He asked his servants to find someone who could play music to help him feel better. One of his servants answered, "There is a son of Jesse named David. He is a skilled and good-natured young man who plays the lyre."

David was sent for and entered the service of King Saul. Saul liked David very much and gave him the role of his armour-bearer. Every time David played the lyre, the music lifted Saul's spirits. David went back and forth from Saul to feed and look after his father's sheep on the hillsides of Bethlehem.

Now the Philistines had once again gathered their army and entered the land of Judah. Saul, leading the Israelite army, went out to stop them. The armies set up camps, facing each other across the valley. There came out of the Philistine camp a giant of a man named Goliath. He looked fierce and strong with a helmet of bronze, a heavy coat of armour, greaves of bronze on his legs, and a bronze javelin slung across his shoulders. He carried a spear and his shield-bearer went before him.

Roaring across the valley, Goliath shouted at the Israelites, "Choose a man to come down to me. If he can fight and kill me, then we will be your servants, but if I kill him then you shall serve us."

When Saul and the Israelites heard these words, they were very afraid. Each morning and evening for forty days, Goliath came forward to roar his challenge.

Jesse's eldest three sons were soldiers in Saul's army. Early one morning, Jesse sent David to take some food to his brothers in the Israelite camp and find out how they were doing. As David talked to his brothers, once again the Philistine champion shouted his words. David was horrified that Goliath was being allowed to humiliate the army of God's people. Saul heard of David's brave talk and summoned him.

David said, "No one should be fearful of this Philistine. I will go and fight him."

Saul was amazed. "You are just a boy, and this Philistine has been a warrior since his youth."

Determined, David replied, "I looked after sheep for my father and whenever a lion or a bear came, I would strike it down and kill it. God who saved me from the paws of the lion and the bear will save me from the hand of this Philistine."

Saul relented and offered David his armour, but he could not walk with it on and was not used to wearing it. So, removing it and putting down Saul's sword, David went down to the valley stream carrying his staff. He chose five smooth stones and put them in his shepherd's bag. With just his sling in his hand, he drew near to Goliath.

As he approached, Goliath scornfully looked at David, shouting, "Do you think that I am a dog for you come to me with sticks? Get closer and I will give your dead body to the birds and wild animals."

David replied, "You come to me with javelin and spear, but I come to you in the name of the God of Israel, who will strike you down."

With that, David took out a stone and placed it into his sling. Throwing it with great skill, the stone flew and with a powerful force struck Goliath on his forehead. The giant fell to the ground, stunned. Running forward, David took Goliath's sword out of its sheath and killed him. When the Philistines saw their champion was dead, they fled. The Israelites surged forward shouting and pursued them.

A Faithful Friendship

1 Samuel 18 – 2 Samuel 1

FROM THAT DAY, Saul wanted David constantly in his presence. Jonathan, Saul's son, became great friends with David and gave him some of his most precious possessions – his armour, sword, bow, and belt. Wherever Saul sent David, the young man was successful and much loved, and praised by the Israelites. Soon Saul was filled with jealousy. One day as David played the lyre, Saul picked up his spear and hurled it at him. David leaped aside. Twice Saul tried to kill David and each time he escaped. Saul was now more afraid of David because God was with him.

Jonathan tried to persuade his father that David's actions had been of good service, but this did not last long. With his life in danger, David fled, but he returned to speak to his friend Jonathan.

"What have I done wrong?" David asked. "Why does your father want to kill me?"

Jonathan was determined to find out if this really was Saul's intention, and they planned a signal to indicate if it was safe for

David to return. David hid in a field nearby as Jonathan dined with his father. When Saul questioned why David's place was empty at the feast, Jonathan replied that he had to return to Bethlehem to be with his family. Saul was enraged and threw a spear at his son. Jonathan knew that his father intended to kill David.

In the morning, greatly saddened, Jonathan went out to the field with his servant. Just as they had agreed, Jonathan shot his arrow and then, as the boy went to fetch it, he called out clearly, "The arrow is further on."

David knew it was no longer safe to return. After sending his servant away, Jonathan returned to the field to say goodbye to his dear friend.

For many years after, David hid from Saul. He was popular with the people and helped them when they were being mistreated. A loyal band of followers gathered around him, and David learned to become a respected leader, guided by God. Samuel died and Saul became a desperate king. On the slopes of Mount Gilboa, the Philistines once again fought with the Israelites, and Saul and his three sons died. News of their deaths reached David in the desert and he mourned them, especially his friend Jonathan.

Psalms of King David

2 Samuel 5–7; Psalms

FOR A WHILE there was turmoil in Israel, but finally the tribes came together and met with David. David was anointed king of Israel at the age of thirty and reigned for forty years. He marched to Jerusalem, a fortress town surrounded by hills with huge city gates. The city belonged to the Jebusites. David sent soldiers up the shaft that supplied the city with water and they unlocked the gates, letting his army in to take the city. Jerusalem became known as the City of David.

With a great procession and celebration, the ark of the Lord's covenant was brought to Jerusalem and set up in a new tabernacle. David intended to build a temple, but the prophet Nathan spoke the words of God to him. "God has taken you from the pasture to being king over the flock of Israel. God will make for you a great name. When your days are fulfilled, God will raise up your son and establish his kingdom. He shall build a house for God. God will not take his steadfast love from him. Your house and your throne shall last for ever."

David was full of praise and thanksgiving and expressed his thoughts and feelings about God through songs and poems. During the difficult times and the wars, he turned to God for strength and shelter.

The Lord is my shepherd, I lack nothing.
He makes me lie down in green pastures,
he leads me beside quiet waters,
he refreshes my soul.
He guides me along the right paths
for his name's sake.
Even though I walk
through the darkest valley,
I will fear no evil,
for you are with me;
your rod and your staff,
they comfort me.

(PSALM 23)

Whoever dwells in the shelter of the Most High
will rest in the shadow of the Almighty.
I will say of the Lord, "He is my refuge and my fortress,
my God, in whom I trust."

Surely he will save you from the fowler's snare
and from the deadly pestilence.
He will cover you with his feathers,
and under his wings you will find refuge;
his faithfulness will be your shield and rampart.

(Psalm 91:1–4)

Praise the Lord.

Praise God in his sanctuary;
praise him in his mighty heavens.
Praise him for his acts of power;
praise him for his surpassing greatness.
Praise him with the sounding of the trumpet,
praise him with the harp and lyre,
praise him with tambourine and dancing,
praise him with the strings and pipe,
praise him with the clash of cymbals,
praise him with resounding cymbals.

Let everything that has breath praise the Lord.

Praise the Lord.

(Psalm 150)

Moments of Kindness and Weakness

2 Samuel 9–18; Psalms

When David was king, he remembered his good friend Jonathan, and asked if there was anyone left in his family. In other lands, usually a new king would put to death all those from a rival house, but David showed that he behaved differently. He discovered that Jonathan's son Mephibosheth was still alive and sent for him. With great fear, Mephibosheth appeared before David. He was unable to walk because when he was young, his nurse had dropped him when fleeing on the news of the death of Saul and his father.

"Do not be afraid," David told him. "I will show you kindness and return to you all the land of your grandfather Saul. You shall live and eat with me here, as if you were my son."

Although David tried to be a good king for God, there were times when he went his own way. On one occasion, he had sent his soldiers to battle with the Ammonites, but he remained comfortably in Jerusalem. Late one afternoon, he walked about on the roof of the palace, looking out over Jerusalem, and saw a very beautiful woman bathing. He inquired about who she was and discovered she was Bathsheba, the wife of a trusted soldier named Uriah. Uriah was away at the battle. David was overwhelmed with a wish to be with Bathsheba and sent for her, committing adultery.

A short while later, Bathsheba sent David a message that she was pregnant. David summoned Uriah back from the battle under the pretence that he wanted news about how the war was going.

Then David told him, "Go to your house and spend time with your wife before you return to the battle."

But Uriah did not go home for he thought of the other soldiers and did not believe it was right that he should have comfort while they were fighting.

In the morning, David wrote a letter to Joab, the general of the army, about Uriah, stating, "Put Uriah where the battle is hardest and then leave him to be killed."

Unknowingly, Uriah carried the letter to Joab. Joab carried out the order and many soldiers died in the attack, including Uriah. Bathsheba mourned the death of her husband, but then David sent for her and she became his wife.

The prophet Nathan went to David and spoke God's message: "I gave you so much: a palace, wives, and children, and I would have given you so much more, but now you have done wrong and trouble will come to your family."

David admitted that he had done wrong, so God forgave him. Bathsheba's child became ill and died, but they had another son, named Solomon. Quarrels arose between David's other sons; one killed another and later tried to take power from David. David knew great sorrow whenever he did wrong, but he always admitted his foolishness and asked for God's forgiveness. God stayed with him.

The Wisdom of King Solomon

1 Kings 1–3; Proverbs; Ecclesiastes

When David became very old and could not leave his room, thoughts turned to who would be the next king. Adonijah was now David's eldest living son, but David wished for his son Solomon to succeed him. When David heard that Adonijah was planning to become king, he summoned the priest Zadok and the prophet Nathan.

He instructed, "Take Solomon riding on my own mule through the city and anoint him king. Blow the trumpet and announce, 'Long live King Solomon!' to all the people."

When Solomon was anointed king, there was much rejoicing. He also did not harm Adonijah.

As his life came to an end, David gave advice to Solomon, saying,

"Be strong and courageous, and follow the guidance of God. Obey the laws given to Moses, and if you do, you will prosper in return. This was promised to me by God."

Once David died, Solomon took on the responsibility of the kingdom of Israel, with its great number of people. One day, he went to the altar at Gibeon to make an offering to God.

That night, God appeared to him in a dream and spoke, saying, "What gift should I give you, Solomon?"

Solomon knew what he wanted most. "O God, you have made me your servant king in place of my father David, although I am still young and inexperienced. Give me wisdom so that I can discern between what is right and wrong and govern your people well."

God was pleased with Solomon's request, saying, "Because you have asked for wisdom, and not for long life and riches for yourself, I will not only give you a wise mind but also riches and success. You will be praised and respected by everyone. If you walk with me, then you will have a long life."

As Solomon dealt with the affairs at court, he found that he had the wisdom that God had promised him. People came to him for wise judgment. His kingdom reached from the River Euphrates to the border of Egypt and was plentiful and the people lived safely.

Jerusalem's Temple

1 Kings 5–10

God gave Solomon great wisdom and other nations came to hear about him. Solomon had knowledge about trees and flowers and all kinds of animals. He composed 3,000 wise sayings called proverbs and wrote a thousand songs.

There was peace in the land, and so Solomon knew this was the time to fulfil his father's plan to build a great house for God. Thousands of workers were involved in preparing the stone for constructing the Temple and bringing the cedar wood that lined the whole of the inside from Lebanon. Craftsmen carved flowers, palm trees, and winged cherubim in the wood. The inner sanctuary of the Temple was to be the place for the ark of the Lord's covenant. Everything was overlaid with gold. The doors of the inner sanctuary were made of olive wood and there were two great entrance doors made of cypress wood. Two pillars of bronze decorated with pomegranates at the top were positioned at the entrance of the Temple. It took seven years to build.

Solomon had all the furnishings for the Temple handcrafted: the golden altar, the golden table for the bread offered to God, ten gold lampstands, the cups and basins, the dishes and the firepans. Everything was brought into the Temple and the vessels that the priests would need were stored in the treasury. When all was ready, Solomon brought together the elders of the tribes of Israel for a great ceremony.

The wonderful moment came when the ark containing the two stone tablets given to Moses was carried by the priests into the inner sanctuary. When the priests came out, a dazzling cloud of God's glorious presence filled the Temple. Solomon was filled with wonder and praise. He knew that God was with them, to bless them and hear their prayers. He encouraged everyone to be devoted to God and keep God's Law. The festival lasted seven days. The people celebrated, then afterwards returned home full of joy.

During this time, Solomon also built a great palace for his court. In the years that followed, he built a great fleet of ships that traded gold, special wood, and precious stones. Kings from other lands came to Jerusalem bearing presents and the queen of Sheba brought a huge quantity of spices as well as gold and precious stones. They all wanted to hear the great wisdom of Solomon in response to their questions, and they were all impressed.

A Divided Kingdom

1 Kings 11–12

ALL SEEMED WELL in Solomon's kingdom, but there was one instruction from God that Solomon had not followed. The Israelites were not to marry people from other lands. Solomon however loved many foreign women and had many hundreds of wives. Instead of guiding them to follow God, Solomon let them worship their own gods. As Solomon grew old, he was influenced by his wives and built shrines for their gods. God was angry because Solomon had turned away.

God spoke to him, saying, "You have not kept my laws as you promised, and so I should take the kingdom away from you. But I promised your father that I would not do this to you. Instead your son will only receive a small part of the kingdom."

Unrest and rebellion began to rise up in the kingdom because Solomon forced people to work for him and made the people pay heavy taxes. One of these rebellions was led by Jeroboam, who was

a good worker and in charge of the workmen repairing the city walls of Jerusalem. He fled to Egypt but returned when news came of Solomon's death. Solomon's son Rehoboam succeeded him and became king of Israel, but the people wanted changes to how they were being treated.

Jeroboam and other elders of Israel's tribes came to speak to Rehoboam.

"Your father treated us harshly. If you treat us kindly and make life easier for the people, then we will serve you loyally."

Rehoboam asked for three days for him to decide what he would do. He asked advice from some older advisers of his father, who told him to rule more gently. He also went to speak to some young courtiers, whom he had grown up with. They gave a very different answer. They suggested that he should treat the people more harshly than his father, and to rule them so firmly that they could not rebel.

Rehoboam followed the advice of the young courtiers. When the tribes of Israel knew that he would not listen to them, they gathered and chose Jeroboam as their king. Only the tribes of Judah and Benjamin chose to follow Rehoboam, and so the great nation was split into two kingdoms, Israel in the north and Judah in the south.

Elijah, the Prophet

1 Kings 12–17

JERUSALEM WAS IN the southern kingdom, and all the Israelites would go to the Temple at least once every year to worship. Jeroboam was concerned that the people from the northern kingdom would turn again to Rehoboam as king. So he ordered two golden calves to be made and built two shrines, one at each end of his kingdom, for them. He announced an annual festival for the people to be held at the shrines. The people quickly turned away from worshipping God and instead made offerings to these images.

One king followed another in Israel, and it seemed that the people of Israel would forget all about God as they followed their own way and abandoned God's Law. King Ahab married Queen Jezebel, who was a princess from a nearby land, and she brought hundreds of prophets of the god Baal to Israel.

But God chose a man to try and remind the people of God's great power and loving protection. This prophet was Elijah, and he was not afraid to speak out.

He boldly went and stood before King Ahab, saying, "In the God of Israel's name, there will be no rain until I give the word."

Without rain, the land quickly dried up, and the harvests failed. Following God's instructions, Elijah came to the house of a widow, who lived with her son. He asked for water and some bread, but the widow in despair said, "I have nothing but a handful of flour and a few drops of oil. I am about to make our last meal to eat."

Elijah reassured her, saying, "Do not be afraid. Make a little loaf for me and then use the rest to make one for yourself and your son. The God of Israel has promised that as long as the drought lasts you will not run out of flour or oil."

The widow did as Elijah asked and there was always enough to feed them.

A while later, the son became so ill that he could hardly breathe. The widow cried out to Elijah, "Have you come to cause the death of my son?"

Elijah carried the boy to the upper room, and cried out to God, "O God have you brought disaster even to this widow that I am staying with? Let this child live once again."

God listened and the boy revived, breathing once again. When the widow saw her son alive, she was overjoyed.

"Now I know you are sent by God," she told Elijah, "and you speak God's words."

The Voice in the Silence

1 Kings 18–19

THE DROUGHT CONTINUED for three years. King Ahab grew desperate. The god Baal was meant to be the god of rain, but none came despite all the prayers of Jezebel's prophets. Ahab sent for Elijah.

Elijah suggested a contest to prove to Ahab that he should not have turned away from the God of Israel. Some 450 prophets of Baal built an altar, but the contest was not to light it with fire but cry out to their god to do this. Despite their wailing and dancing and rituals for many hours, the altar to Baal was not lit.

Elijah then built an altar, and even drenched everything with water. When he made the offering to God, the fire of the Lord lit the altar, consuming everything. The people threw themselves to the ground, amazed at the incredible power of God. The prophets of Baal were killed, and Elijah was overjoyed as rain began to fall.

When Jezebel heard about what had happened, she swore to kill Elijah. So Elijah fled. He journeyed far into the wilderness for forty days until he reached the mountain in Sinai. He felt alone and afraid for he was the only prophet of God left in Israel. There was a great wind, but God was not present. Then followed an earthquake and a fire, but God was still not there. Then there was the sound of complete silence.

Elijah heard the voice of God, saying, "Go back; there is work still to be done. Find Elisha to follow you, for he will be my prophet after you. There are still 7,000 people in Israel who have never worshipped Baal."

Encouraged, Elijah found Elisha ploughing in his family's field. Elijah threw his cloak over Elisha to show that he would be the next prophet, and Elisha said goodbye to his family and went with him.

Naboth's Vineyard

1 Kings 21 – 2 Kings 2

BESIDE THE PALACE of King Ahab was a vineyard owned by a man named Naboth. Ahab wanted the vineyard to make a vegetable garden and requested the land from Naboth, promising a larger vineyard elsewhere. Naboth was unable to sell because it was against God's Law to give away the land inherited and passed down through his family. Ahab sulked for not getting his own way. His wife Jezebel was surprised when Ahab told her why he sulked.

"Are you not the king of Israel?" she replied. "Be cheerful, for you shall have the vineyard."

Jezebel sent letters in Ahab's name to elders and the city's nobles, stating that Naboth should be accused of treason against the king and had cursed God. The charges against Naboth were brought to the assembly and he was stoned to death. When Ahab heard that Naboth was dead, he took the vineyard, breaking God's Law.

God sent Elijah to Ahab with a warning. "Because you have killed and taken possession of another's inheritance, your own blood will be spilled, Jezebel will die, and your family destroyed."

Ahab was horrified at what he had done, and repented, trying to change his ways. But this did not last long. He was killed in battle, and there continued to be kings of Israel who were unfaithful to God.

At the end of his life, Elijah was with Elisha at the River Jordan near Jericho. As Elijah struck the river, the water parted, and they crossed on dry ground. As they walked and talked, a chariot of fire pulled by fiery horses separated them and Elijah ascended in a whirlwind into heaven. Elisha picked up Elijah's cloak to continue his work as a prophet.

Stories of Elisha

2 Kings 4

God was with Elisha and he was able to perform amazing works through the power of the word of God. A widow with two children came to him, desperate for his help. She had debts, and if she were unable to pay, her two children would be taken and sold as slaves.

Elisha asked her, "What do you have in the house?"

"Nothing except a jar of oil," the widow replied.

"Go to those who live nearby," Elisha told her, "and ask to borrow their empty jars. Then shut the door and start pouring the oil that you have into them."

Those who lived nearby kept bringing their jars and she kept pouring. When there were no more jars to be filled, the oil stopped flowing. Elisha then told her to sell the oil to pay her debts, and the remaining money would be enough for her and her children to live on.

Elisha journeyed from place to place, teaching people to live in God's way. In Shumen, a wealthy woman invited Elisha to have a meal, and told him to return whenever he was passing. She and her husband even built an extra room on the flat roof of the house for Elisha to stay in. Elisha was grateful and wondered what could be done for them. He found out that they had everything they wanted, except for a child.

Elisha called for the woman, telling her, "This time next year, you will have a son to hold."

This came true. One day though, when the child was older and with his father and the reapers in the fields, he complained to his father of having a headache. One of the servants carried him home, but by noon, the child had died. His mother carried him up to Elisha's room, and then set out on a donkey to find Elisha.

When Elisha heard the news, he returned with her to Shumen, and saw the child lying dead on his bed. He closed the door and prayed to God. He laid over the child, and the boy's body started to grow warm. Then the child sneezed seven times and opened his eyes, alive and healthy once more.

The Healing of Naaman

2 Kings 5

NAAMAN WAS A commander of the Aramean army. He was wealthy and was greatly respected by the king of Aram. But he also had a terrible skin disease called leprosy and, at that time, there was no cure. On one of the Aramean raids into Israel they had captured a young girl, who now served Naaman's wife.

She told her mistress, "There is a prophet in Israel who could heal my master."

Offering silver, gold, and silks to Israel's king, the king of Aram arranged for Naaman to safely visit Elisha. When Naaman arrived, Elisha sent out his messenger with instructions, saying, "My master tells you to wash yourself in the Jordan seven times, and your skin will be cured."

Naaman was disappointed and angry that Elisha had not appeared and cured his leprosy with a wave of his hand. There were cleaner rivers in his country. Elisha's messenger persuaded him to at least give it a try.

As he dipped himself seven times, Naaman's skin was completely healed. Naaman returned to Elisha to thank him, and declared, "Now I know that the God of Israel is the only true God in the world."

Elisha was famous for being a prophet of God. He was feared by foreign kings, but they also came to him for advice. He helped the people, too. After he died, there continued to be many struggles in the northern kingdom of Israel. The kings and the people often did not follow God's ways and there were wars and rebellions. Despite many warnings to the people of Israel to turn back to worshipping God, they did not listen.

Jonah, the Reluctant Prophet

Jonah 1

IN THE REIGN of King Jeroboam II, there was a man named Jonah who lived near Nazareth in Israel. God chose him to send a message, not to the people of Israel but to those in the capital city of nearby Assyria. The Assyrians were known for their injustice and cruelty to people who were captured or outcasts. They were the greatest threat to Israel's nation.

God spoke to Jonah, saying, "Go to the great city of Nineveh, and tell the people that I know about their wickedness. Tell them to change their ways."

Jonah was horrified by God's request. He knew that if they changed their ways, God would not punish them. So he journeyed in the opposite direction toward the port of Joppa, wishing to cross the Mediterranean Sea to Tarshish in Spain and flee from God's presence.

When the ship was at sea, God sent a great wind to whip up a mighty storm. The sailors were afraid that the ship would break up and they cried out to their gods. They threw their cargo overboard to try to gain more control, but without success. Meanwhile, Jonah was fast asleep below deck.

The captain woke him, asking, "What are you doing asleep? Call out to your God to save us."

The sailors believed there was someone onboard who had angered their god, so they cast lots to find out who this might be. The lot fell on Jonah.

"Why did this calamity happen to us?" they asked him. "Where do you come from?"

Jonah told them, "I am from Israel and I worship the Lord God of heaven, who made the sea and the land. I am fleeing from his presence."

The sailors were very afraid of him and asked, "What shall we do to you so that the sea will calm?" For the sea was getting rougher and rougher.

"Throw me into the sea," Jonah instructed them, "for I know it is because of me that this storm has happened."

The sailors were reluctant and instead tried to row the ship back to land, but they could not as the storm became more violent. They prayed to Jonah's God, crying out, "Please do not make us guilty of taking an innocent man's life."

Then they picked up Jonah and threw him into the sea. Immediately the sea calmed, and the sailors were amazed at God's power.

A City Saved

Jonah 1–4

As Jonah sank, God sent a large fish to swallow him and for three days and three nights, Jonah stayed in the belly of the fish. Alone in the dark, Jonah prayed to God, saying sorry for disobeying, and giving thanks for being rescued. God then gave word to the fish, and it spat Jonah out onto the land.

God spoke again to Jonah, saying, "Get up and go to Nineveh and tell them that in forty days I shall destroy the city."

This time, Jonah walked for three days, arrived in Nineveh, and proclaimed God's message. The people believed him, even the king, and everyone in the city was told to fast and wear sackcloth to show that they were sorry for how they had behaved so violently toward others. Even the animals were given nothing and covered in sackcloth. The people hoped that this would be enough to change the mind of God. It was, and God decided not to destroy the city.

Jonah was angered by God's decision and sat down outside the city, feeling miserable. He prayed, "I knew you were a kind, loving God, slow to anger, and would not punish them. That is why I ran away. So now, just let me die!"

But God did not let Jonah die. Instead, he made a plant grow to shade him from the burning sun. Jonah felt happier. The next day, the plant was attacked by a worm, withered, and died, and once again the sun burned down on Jonah. Jonah was upset about the plant.

"You are concerned about a plant that you did not even grow or care for," God said to him. "Do you not think I have the right to be concerned about the people of Nineveh and the many animals? I gave them life and care about them."

Jonah began to understand, and in the years following, the Assyrians became more powerful, while Israel's kings turned further away from God.

A later king of Assyria invaded Israel's land. The Assyrians came to live in the cities of Samaria and the people of Israel were taken to Assyria. They brought their gods and mixed them with worshipping God.

King Josiah's Reforms

2 Kings 18–23

The Assyrians continued to march on, attacking the southern kingdom of Judah. The people of Judah had also turned away from worshipping God and following God's Law. But at that time their king, Hezekiah, was a good man who trusted God. They also had a prophet named Isaiah, who encouraged the people to love and obey God, and to not be afraid for God was with them. The Assyrians reached the gates of Jerusalem, but then disaster struck in their camp one night. Thousands of Assyrian soldiers died. The king of Assyria withdrew his army, as there was also news that his own country was being invaded.

Although there was peace for a while in Judah, all was not well. After Hezekiah's death, other kings of Judah followed their own selfish ways and the people once again made images of gods to worship and even killed their own children, offering them as sacrifices.

King Josiah was only eight years old when he became king. When he was eighteen, he gave orders to repair God's Temple in Jerusalem. An old book was found and given to the high priest, who passed it to the king's secretary. The secretary showed it to Josiah and read it to him. In despair, Josiah realized it was the book of God's Law, which had been forgotten. He sent the priests to find out what he and the people must do.

The priests went to God's prophetess, Huldah, and she told them, "God has said that the people of Judah will suffer because they have abandoned God's ways. But as the king of Judah is humbled, this will not happen in his lifetime."

Josiah sent for the elders of Judah and gathered the people, the priests, and the prophets in Jerusalem. In front of the Temple, the king read out the laws to them and promised God that these commands would be followed. The people joined in the covenant. A great reform of the country took place, in which all the images of other gods and anything to do with worshipping them were destroyed. Once this was done, for the first time in hundreds of years, a Passover festival was celebrated, remembering God bringing the people out from Egypt.

The Fall of Jerusalem

2 Kings 24–25; Jeremiah 26–39

The small kingdom of Judah was caught between the surrounding great nations to the south and north. In the north, the Babylonians were invading the Assyrians' land. To the south, the king of Egypt wanted to support the Assyrians in their fight, but this meant marching through Judah. Sadly, Josiah was killed in battle trying to stop the Egyptians. The king of Egypt then imposed heavy taxes on the people of Judah, but this did not stop the Babylonians from advancing. King Nebuchadnezzar of Babylon won a decisive victory and forced Egypt to retreat. The people of Judah and its king were now in the control of the Babylonians, and they had to pay taxes to them.

There was a prophet named Jeremiah, who wanted to warn the people that unless they turned back to God terrible things would happen. He stood at the gates of the city of Jerusalem telling people about God's Law. He went to the Temple in Jerusalem to warn people that the city and the Temple would be destroyed for God would abandon them if they abandoned God. Jeremiah was very unpopular and thrown into a well.

The Babylonians were at the gates of Jerusalem and the people inside the city were running out of food. An Ethiopian man named Ebed-Melek went to King Zedekiah to ask for help in rescuing Jeremiah. Ebed-Melek was given three men to help him lower some ropes and some old rags and worn-out clothes down to Jeremiah to lift him out of the well.

The king asked for some advice from Jeremiah. He advised, "Surrender and then your life will be spared. If not, the city will be destroyed."

But King Zedekiah ignored his advice. The city was taken, and the Temple was burned down. All the treasures inside the Temple were taken to Babylon, and some of the Israelites from noble families were sent to serve in King Nebuchadnezzar's palace.

Exiled in Babylon

Daniel 1–3

Among the young men taken to serve in the king of Babylon's palace were Daniel, Hananiah, Mishael, and Azariah from the tribe of Judah. They were to be taught the literature and language of the country and educated in the ways of the Babylonians. They were given different names: Belteshazzar, Shadrach, Meshach, and Abednego. They were to eat the palace food of meat and wine, but they were determined to follow God's Law.

Daniel told the palace master, "Allow us to eat vegetables and water for ten days. Then compare our appearance to your other servants."

After ten days, the palace master could see that the four young men were healthier than those who had been eating the palace food, so he allowed them to continue eating the food they wanted.

One night, King Nebuchadnezzar had a dream that troubled him. None of his advisors could tell him what his dream was or what it meant. God revealed the dream to Daniel and its meaning. He was brought before the king.

"Your dream was of a huge frightening statue with its head made of gold, its chest and arms of silver, its middle and thighs of bronze, its legs of iron, and its feet of iron and clay. As you watched a stone not carved by human hands struck the statue and it broke into pieces. You, O king, rule the kingdom that represents the head of gold. Other kingdoms will come after, but the God of heaven will set up a kingdom that shall never be destroyed. It will crush all the kingdoms and will stand for ever."

Daniel was promoted in the king's court and Nebuchadnezzar was so proud that he ordered a huge golden statue to be built. Everyone was sent for and ordered to bow down and worship the statue when they heard the sound of the horns and other instruments.

Shadrach, Meshach, and Abednego were determined to follow God's Law and did not bow down.

In a furious rage, Nebuchadnezzar ordered them to be thrown into a fiery furnace. They were bound and lifted into the furnace, which was so hot that it scorched the men throwing them in. As the king watched he was astonished, for he saw four people unbound in the fire and none were hurt. He ordered the men to bring them out of the fire. Shadrach, Meshach, and Abednego were amazingly unharmed. The king praised their God and proclaimed that no one should say a word against their God.

The Lions' Den

Daniel 5–6

After the reign of Nebuchadnezzar, his son Belshazzar ruled. One night he held a great feast, and his guests drank from the gold and silver cups that had been taken from the Temple of Jerusalem. As they celebrated, a human hand appeared and began writing on the wall. King Belshazzar was terrified. He sent for advisors to interpret the writing on the wall, but they could not. Daniel, who was now an elderly man, was called for and offered gifts for interpreting the writing.

Daniel answered, "Keep your gifts, but I will interpret the writing. When your father recognized the Most High God, he was given greatness, but when his heart hardened his kingdom was stripped away. This hand was sent from God and the writing MENE TEKEL PARSIN means that your days are numbered, you have been found wanting, and your kingdom will be divided."

That night, Darius the Mede raided the palace with his Persian army and Belshazzar was killed. Daniel was given responsibility as one of three chief rulers, who oversaw the local rulers of the vast Persian kingdom. The other rulers were displeased that Daniel was regarded so highly, so they planned a way to have him killed. They persuaded King Darius to sign a command that whoever prayed to anyone other than him for thirty days would be thrown to the lions.

Daniel knew the document had been signed, but he continued to kneel three times a day to pray and praise God in front of an open window that faced in the direction of Jerusalem. Darius was informed, and he was greatly distressed for he respected and valued Daniel. Unable to take back his command, Daniel was thrown into the den of lions.

The king said to Daniel, "May your God, whom you faithfully serve, deliver you."

The king didn't eat and was restless all night, and at the break of the new day, he hurried to the den. When he was near, he cried anxiously, "O Daniel, servant of the living God, were you saved from the lions?"

To his wonder and relief, the king heard Daniel reply.

"Yes," called Daniel, "my God sent a messenger to shut the lions' mouths as I had done nothing wrong, and I have not been harmed."

The king was overjoyed and commanded Daniel to be taken out of the den. He then made a new law, declaring, "Let everyone in my kingdom know the power of the God of Daniel, who lives for ever and performs signs and wonders in heaven and on earth."

The Return from Exile

Ezra; Nehemiah

Although God's people had been scattered during the exile, God had not forgotten them, and he stirred up the mind of the new king of Persia, Cyrus. In his first year, Cyrus proclaimed that God's people, now known as the Jews, could return to Jerusalem, taking with them the treasures that had been stolen from the Temple and rebuild the city. More than 42,000 people journeyed back across the desert to Jerusalem, taking with them everything that they owned. In their years away from their land, they had learned to love and trust God once more.

When the Jews arrived, their first plan was to rebuild the Temple and they gave gifts of gold and silver to fund the work. As the builders laid the foundations, the priests praised God, blowing trumpets and crashing cymbals as King David had done many, many years before. The people living in the land offered help to the returning exiles, because they also worshipped God. The Jewish people refused their offer, but this caused unrest and the building work was delayed. God's prophets, Haggai and Zechariah, spoke out, reminding people to not look at their own needs but to refocus on building God's Temple. Work began again and there was a great celebration when the Temple was completed.

A priest named Ezra, who had studied in Babylon, helped the Jews learn once more about God's Law so that they would become faithful to God and look after the land and each other. Ezra particularly stopped them from marrying women from other nations, so that they would become strong once again. Also returning from Babylon was a governor named Nehemiah. He set about restoring the city walls of Jerusalem, organizing the building work. The people living in the land were afraid that Jerusalem would become a strong walled city again, so they tried to stop the work by discouraging the Jews. Nehemiah prayed for God's help to protect them as the work continued. It took fifty-two days to rebuild the walls and the Jews held a great celebration, rejoicing and praising God. The joy of Jerusalem was heard far away.

Esther, the Chosen Queen

Esther 1–4

IN THE TIME of the great Persian empire, King Xerxes held a great banquet to celebrate his wealth and success. He commanded his wife Queen Vashti, who was holding a banquet for the women, to join the men so he could display her beauty, but she refused. In punishment, her position as the queen was removed from her. The king appointed commissioners to find him another beautiful lady to be his queen.

There was a Jewish man in the city named Mordecai and he cared for his cousin, Esther, for she had no parents. Esther was selected as one of the beautiful women to be presented to the king. Mordecai told her to tell no one that she was Jewish. Esther was admired not just for her beauty but also for her humility and obedience. The king chose her to be his queen.

One day Mordecai was at the palace gates and overheard a plot to assassinate the king. He told this to Queen Esther, and she told the king, saying the information had come from Mordecai. The plot was found to be true and the details recorded.

There was an official named Haman, whom the king set above all the others. All the king's servants and officials were expected to bow before him. But Mordecai did not, because this was against God's Law. When Haman heard this, he was enraged and plotted to destroy all the Jewish people throughout the whole of the Persian empire. He spoke to the king about the Jewish people scattered across his kingdom, who followed their own laws and did not keep the king's laws. Haman was given authority by the king to do with them whatever he thought best. In the king's name, Haman sent letters to every province setting the date for all Jews, young and old, to be killed.

When Mordecai learned of this news, he wept and mourned, as did all the Jews across the kingdom. Esther was greatly distressed when she heard from Mordecai about what would happen to her and her people. Mordecai wanted her to plead to the king. However, she knew she could only go to the king if she was summoned by him. She would be put to death unless the king held out his golden staff.

Mordecai wrote to her, saying, "Perhaps you have been made queen for such a time as this."

The Courageous Request

Esther 5–10

FOLLOWING MORDECAI'S LETTER, Esther bravely decided to go before the king. After three days of praying and fasting, she put on her royal robes and went to the inner court of the king's palace. The king spied her and held out his golden staff so that Esther could approach.

"What is your request, Queen Esther?" the king asked.

"If it pleases the king, I have prepared a banquet today for you and Haman."

The king was overjoyed and summoned Haman to the banquet. At the meal, the king said, "Whatever you request I will grant to you."

Esther invited them both to a banquet the next day to say her request. Haman left the banquet delighted, but at the palace's gate he saw Mordecai and this dampened his good spirits. His wife suggested that he built some gallows from which to hang him, and this delighted Haman, so the gallows were made.

That night, the king was unable to sleep so he read the book that contained the details of the thwarted assassination plot. He asked his servants, "What gift was given to Mordecai for saving my life?"

"Nothing has been done for him," the servants replied.

He summoned Haman and asked him, "What gift should be given for a man I wish to praise?"

Thinking the king was talking about him, Haman replied, "Let him wear royal robes that you have worn, be given a horse that you have ridden and a royal crown, and let him ride through the city, proclaiming, 'The king wishes to praise this man.'"

The king was delighted with this idea and instructed Haman to robe Mordecai in this way and lead his horse around the city, proclaiming. Haman did this and returned home mournfully before being summoned to Queen Esther's banquet.

At the feast, the king once again promised to grant whatever she requested.

Queen Esther answered, "If I please you, O king, let my life and the lives of my people be spared, for we are to be killed and annihilated."

The king was shocked, asking, "Who is he and where is he, the one who presumes to do this?"

Queen Esther pointed to Haman, saying, "This wicked Haman!"

Haman was terrified. The king rose angrily and went out to think. Haman pleaded with Esther, but when the king returned, he ordered Haman to be hanged on the gallows that had been prepared for Mordecai.

The king gave Haman's household to Esther, and Haman's position was given to Mordecai. The king permitted new letters to be written to the provinces to cancel the previous orders to kill all the Jewish people. These were sent out quickly, and in every area, the Jews rejoiced and celebrated with a new festival, the feast of Purim. God's people had been saved.

THIS PART OF the Bible contains twenty-seven books. They begin with four accounts of the life and teachings of Jesus, then go on to tell the story of how the wonderful good news about Jesus spreads. Many books are letters to the newly formed churches, providing guidance and encouragement as followers of Jesus. This "New" part is about how Jesus, God's Son, came to bring a new everlasting covenant between God and all people everywhere. The Bible ends with a radiant vision of the future new heaven and new earth. This is a selection of some of the wondrous stories.

The New Testament

A Promised King

Luke 1

GOD LOVED THE world but because Adam and Eve were banished from the garden of Eden, the people were separated from God. God's people, the descendants of Abraham, Isaac, and Jacob, had been chosen to show God's power and protection in the world. But they had not always been faithful to following God's Law, and their land was conquered by other nations. God's prophets proclaimed that God had not abandoned them, and God promised a wonderful king above all other kings. God's promised king would be a redeemer, who would suffer for the wrongs of all people, freeing them so that all people could live for ever with God. The prophets foretold that this messiah would be a descendant of the great King David. The Jewish people waited expectantly for this messiah.

In the time of King Herod, the Jews were under foreign rule once again. Their land was now part of the Roman empire. There was a priest named Zechariah, who served at the Temple in Jerusalem. His wife was a descendant of Moses' brother, Aaron, and her name was Elizabeth. They dearly wished for a child, but now they were both getting old.

One day when Zechariah was on duty, he was chosen to enter the inner sanctuary to offer incense while everyone was praying outside. As he made the offering, a messenger of God appeared. Zechariah was terrified.

"Do not be afraid, Zechariah," the messenger said. "God has heard your prayer. Your wife Elizabeth will bear you a son and you will name him John. Many will rejoice at his birth for he will be filled with God's Spirit. He will prepare the people for God's promised king."

Zechariah was overwhelmed with disbelief. "How will I know that this will happen?" he asked.

"I am Gabriel," replied God's messenger. "I stand in God's presence and have been sent to bring you this good news. Because you did not believe my words, you will be unable to speak until the day this will happen."

Outside the Temple, people were waiting for Zechariah, and wondered why he had been delayed. When Zechariah came out, he could not speak. The people saw this and realized he had seen a vision. Returning home, Elizabeth wondered about his silence.

After this, Elizabeth became pregnant. She was filled with wonder and gave thanks to God.

Chosen Parents

Luke 1

Six months later, God's messenger Gabriel was sent to a town called Nazareth in Galilee. In this town was a young woman named Mary, who was engaged to a man named Joseph, a descendant of King David. Gabriel visited Mary, saying, "Greetings, special one! The Lord is with you."

Mary was worried and fearful.

"Do not be afraid, Mary," said Gabriel. "You have been chosen by God to bear a son. You will name him Jesus. He will be great and called the Son of God. God will give to him the throne of his ancestor David and his kingdom will have no end."

Mary wondered how this would be possible as she wasn't yet married.

"God's Spirit will come upon you," Gabriel said to her, "so this child will be holy. Visit your relative Elizabeth, for in her old age she will also have a son. For nothing is impossible with God."

Mary set out to visit Elizabeth and greeted her as she entered the house. When Elizabeth heard Mary's greeting, the baby within her leaped for joy.

"You are blessed, Mary," Elizabeth cried.

Mary was filled with wonder that she had been chosen to be the mother of God's Son, and she rejoiced. She stayed a while with Elizabeth.

When Joseph heard that Mary was to have a child he was distressed, for he knew that the baby was not his. As he slept, God's messenger appeared to him in a dream, saying, "Joseph, do not be afraid to marry Mary. She will bear a son, and you are to name him Jesus. He will be God's promised redeemer – Emmanuel, which means 'God with us'."

Joseph married Mary and they began to prepare for the child's birth.

Meanwhile, Elizabeth gave birth to a son and all her relatives were pleased. They began talking about the naming the child, suggesting his father's name. But Zechariah shook his head and requested a writing tablet. To everyone's surprise, he wrote, "His name is John."

At that moment, Zechariah was able to speak again. He praised God, saying, "Blessed be God for he has raised a mighty redeemer for us, and this child will go before him to prepare his way."

A Humble Birth

Luke 2

As the time for the birth of Mary's child drew near, the Roman emperor ordered everyone in his empire to return to their hometown to register their name. The emperor wished to make sure that everyone was paying their taxes. Joseph was a descendant of the family of David, so he had to return to the city of Bethlehem. He went to register with Mary, but when they arrived in Bethlehem all the inns were full.

Needing rest after the journey, they found a place among the animals. When Mary's son was born, she wrapped him in bands of cloth to protect him and keep him warm. She used the manger the animals ate from as a bed of straw for her child and laid him down to sleep.

In the fields near Bethlehem, shepherds were keeping watch over their flock. They looked after them day and night, protecting them from any attack by wild animals. On the same night that the child was born, God's messenger appeared before the shepherds, shining in a glow of glorious light. The shepherds were terrified.

"Do not be afraid," God's messenger proclaimed, "for I am bringing you good news of great joy for all people. This day, God's redeemer, the messiah, has been born in the city of David. As a sign, you will find the child wrapped in bands of cloth and lying in a manger."

Suddenly the sky above the shepherds was filled with a heaven-sent host of angels, praising God and saying, "Glory to God in the highest heaven and peace on earth to those blessed by God."

Amazed by what they had heard, the shepherds were eager to find the newborn child and hurried to Bethlehem. There they found the baby lying in the manger just as they had been told, and praised God joyfully. They shared with Mary and Joseph all that they had seen and heard. Mary treasured these words. What a wonder that God's promised king was born in such humble surroundings!

Presented in the Temple

Luke 2

Mary and Joseph named the child Jesus, just as God's messenger had told them. As required by Jewish law for firstborn sons, they took him to Jerusalem's Temple to be dedicated to God.

While they were in the Temple, a faithful old man named Simeon came to meet them. The Spirit of God had revealed to him that before he died, he would see God's messiah. When he saw Jesus, he knew this to have come true.

He took Jesus in his arms and praised God: "You have kept your promise. Now I can rest in peace for I have seen your redeemer, a light showing the way to all and who will bring glory to your people."

Then an elderly wise lady named Anna, who spent all her time in the Temple worshipping, came to meet them. She began to praise God and tell everyone that this was the child that God had promised to them. Mary and Joseph were amazed at the words of Anna and Simeon and thought about them as they returned to Bethlehem.

The Guiding Star

Matthew 2

A NEW BRIGHT STAR appeared in the sky when Jesus was born. This was noticed by wise men from the East, who found meaning in the study of stars. They knew about the prophecies of the Jewish people, passed down from when the Israelites were exiled to foreign lands. When they saw the rising of a new star, they knew this was a sign that the promised king of the Jews had been born. They set out to pay respect to the child, taking gifts with them.

The wise men followed the star and arrived in Jerusalem at the palace of King Herod, whom the Romans had made king of the Jews. When the wise men told Herod about the star and its meaning, Herod was greatly troubled. He called the chief priests of the Temple and the teachers of God's Law, asking them to search the writing of the prophets to find out where the messiah was to be born.

They reported back saying, "God's prophets proclaim that a ruler, who would be the shepherd of God's people, will be born in Bethlehem."

On hearing this news, Herod secretively summoned the wise men, and found out exactly when the star appeared. Then he sent them to

Bethlehem, adding, "Go and search for the child, and when you have found him, let me know so I may visit and worship him as well."

The wise men rode on to Bethlehem, and ahead of them went the star until it stopped over the place where Jesus, Mary, and Joseph were staying. They were overwhelmed with joy. When they entered the house, the wise men kneeled before the young child and offered him their gifts. These were strange gifts for a young child. There was gold for a king, sweet-smelling frankincense used by a priest, and myrrh, which was a spicy ointment used for burying the dead.

In a dream, the wise men were warned not to return to Herod. He was jealous and wished to harm the child, who threatened his power. The wise men journeyed back by another route.

God's messenger also appeared to Joseph in a dream, warning, "King Herod plans to search for Jesus and harm him, so flee to Egypt until the danger has passed."

Joseph immediately woke Mary and the child, packed a few things, and left Bethlehem that night. They journeyed across the desert to Egypt.

When Herod realized that the wise men had not sent any message, he was furious. He ordered his soldiers to kill all the children in and around Bethlehem that were under two years old. No one forgot that terrible day, and Herod was hated by the people.

Only when Herod died did God's messenger return to speak to Joseph in a dream, saying it was now safe to return to Israel. Joseph and Mary took Jesus home to Nazareth.

In My Father's House

Luke 2

JESUS GREW AND became strong, filled with wisdom. God loved him and Jesus learned about God. Every year, Mary and Joseph went to Jerusalem for the Passover festival. When Jesus was twelve years old, he went with them as usual.

After the festival was finished, everyone from other towns and cities started on their way home. After a day's journey, Mary and Joseph suddenly realized that Jesus was not among their group of friends and relatives. They returned to Jerusalem to search for him, worried about his safety and where he might be.

After three days, they retraced their steps to the Temple. There was Jesus sitting among the teachers of God's Law, listening to their responses to his questions. The teachers were amazed at his understanding and his answers.

When Mary and Joseph saw him, they were astonished and relieved. Mary, having been so anxious, asked, "Why have you treated us like this? We have been searching for you and been so worried."

Jesus replied calmly, "Why were you searching for me? Did you know that I must be in my Father's house?"

Mary did not understand what his words meant, but Jesus went with them back to Nazareth. He was always obedient to them as he had been before. He was wise, kind, and loving, and he was loved by everyone.

John the Baptist

Matthew 3; Mark 1; Luke 3; John 1

The son of Zechariah and Elizabeth had also grown in wisdom and learned about God, the laws, and the words of the prophets. When he was older, he lived in the wilderness, dressed in clothing made from camel's hair, and ate locusts and wild honey. He had received a message from God to prepare people for the coming of God's promised king and his kingdom. Crowds of people gathered to hear him speak on the banks of the River Jordan.

He proclaimed, "Repent, for the kingdom of heaven has come near."

John baptized those who came forward by dipping them into the river as a sign that their wrongdoings were washed away.

People asked him about how they should act. John told them to share their clothes with those who had none and share their food with those who were hungry. John told the tax collectors not to cheat and the soldiers not to threaten to take others' money. The people began to wonder if John was God's promised king.

When asked, John replied, "There is one more powerful than I am, who is coming. I baptize you with water, but he will baptize you with the Spirit of God."

One day as John was baptizing people in the river, Jesus came to be baptized. As Jesus approached, John knew he was God's promised king.

"I should be baptized by you," John said to him.

Jesus replied, "It is right that you should baptize me in this way for now."

John dipped Jesus into the water and as he came up again, the heavens suddenly opened and the Spirit of God descended on Jesus like a dove.

A powerful voice spoke, saying, "This is my Son, whom I love dearly. I am pleased with you."

Tempted

Matthew 4; Luke 4

After this, Jesus went into the wilderness to prepare himself for God's work. He ate nothing for forty days and forty nights, and when he was weak from hunger, he was put to the test.

The tempter, who would try to turn Jesus away from God, came to him, saying, "If you are the Son of God, command these stones to become loaves of bread so that you can eat."

Jesus resisted, replying, "It is written: we do not live by bread alone, but by God's words."

The tempter took him to a high spot with a view over Jerusalem.

"If you are the Son of God," said the tempter, "throw yourself down, for God will send angels to lift you up."

Jesus resisted again, saying, "It is written: do not put God to the test."

A third time, the tempter tested him, taking him to a very high mountain from where he could see all the kingdoms of the world.

"All these kingdoms I will give you if you worship me," promised the tempter.

Jesus cried out, "Away with you! It is written: worship and serve God only."

The tempter left him for he could not make Jesus disobey God. Filled with the power of the Spirit, Jesus set out for the region of Galilee, ready for the work that lay ahead.

In the Synagogue

Matthew 4; Luke 4

Jesus had a message of good news from God to share with people. "God's kingdom has come," he told them, "so turn away from everything that is wrong for a new beginning."

Jesus spoke in the synagogues where the Jewish people gathered to worship. His words were inspiring, and crowds began to gather around him to hear him speak and teach with authority. He explained things clearly to them and in a fresh new way.

When he came to Nazareth, where he had been brought up, Jesus went to the synagogue on the sabbath day. He read words by the prophet Isaiah from the scroll of the Jewish holy writings: "The Spirit of God is upon me, because God has anointed me to bring good news to the poor, release those who feel imprisoned by their wrongs, give sight to the blind, free those who are treated unfairly, and to announce the time when God will show kindness to all."

Jesus rolled up the scroll and sat down. Everyone in the synagogue was looking at him.

Then Jesus said to them, "Today these words have come true."

They were amazed but also disbelieving. Jesus was known to them as the kind son of Joseph the local carpenter and had no training for teaching in the synagogue. Jesus knew it would be hard for them to listen to his words. They threw him out of the town, so Jesus went on to the towns and villages nearby.

Calling the First Disciples

Matthew 4; Luke 5; John 1

One day Jesus stood beside the vast Lake Galilee, talking to the gathered crowd. The people began to press closer to hear his words. So Jesus spoke to some fishermen nearby, who were washing their nets, and asked if he could use one of their boats. One fisherman named Simon Peter took him out a little way from the shore in his boat, so that Jesus could sit down and continue teaching the people.

After he had finished speaking, Jesus said to Peter and his brother Andrew, "Take the boat out into deep water and let down your nets."

Peter replied, "We have worked all night but have caught no fish. But if you say so, I will let down the nets."

When Peter and Andrew began to pull in the nets, there were so many fish that the nets were beginning to break. Two other fishermen, brothers James and John, came in their boat to help. The amount of fish caught filled both their boats. They were amazed and would not need to catch fish again for quite some time.

Peter was overwhelmed and kneeled before Jesus.

Jesus said to them all, "Do not be afraid. Follow me and you will become fishers of people."

After bringing their boats to shore, they immediately left everything and went with Jesus.

A man named Philip, who was from the same town as Andrew and Peter, came to Jesus and he brought Nathanael with him.

When Jesus saw Nathanael, he said, "Here comes a kind, honest man."

Nathanael asked, "How do you know me?"

Jesus replied, "I saw you sitting under the fig tree before Philip invited you to come and see me."

Amazed at Jesus' words about his inner thoughts, Nathanael cried, "Teacher! You are the Son of God."

"Follow me," Jesus said to him, "and you will see greater things than this."

The Wedding at Cana

John 2

There was a wedding at a town called Cana in Galilee. Mary and Jesus were invited along with his friends. Wedding celebrations were large events, and there always needed to be plenty of wine. Mary noticed that the wine had run out and knew this would embarrass the bridegroom, so she went and told Jesus.

Then she said to the servants, "Do whatever he tells you."

There were six very large stone water jars nearby that were used by people to wash before the meal, as the Jewish law said. Jesus told the servants to fill the jars with water.

When the jars were filled to the brim, Jesus instructed them, "Pour some out and take it to the steward in charge of organizing the feast."

The servants nervously did as he said. The steward tasted it and then said to the bridegroom, "Everyone serves the best wine first and keeps the ordinary wine for later. But you have kept the best wine until now."

The servants were amazed for they knew that Jesus had turned the water into wine.

Choosing the Twelve

Luke 5–6

As Jesus moved from place to place, people began to follow him. They wanted to hear more about God's kingdom, and how they could become part of this by turning away from their wrongdoings. There was a tax collector named Matthew in the town of Capernaum. One day as he sat collecting the taxes from the farmers, merchants, and traders, Jesus came to him.

"Follow me," Jesus said to him.

Matthew stood up, left everything, and followed him. He gave a great banquet in his house. Many of Matthew's friends were other tax collectors, who often overcharged. The religious leaders, called the Pharisees, were shocked that Jesus was with them.

"Why do you eat and drink with sinners?" the Pharisees complained.

Jesus replied, "Those who are well do not need a doctor. I am like a doctor, for I have come to bring these people back to be with God."

Jesus not only spoke to the people about the good news of the coming of God's kingdom, but also healed people who had diseases. Jesus had God's power to forgive and heal and this amazed the people. His fame spread and the crowds grew. Jesus knew that he needed help with his work to reach more people.

At night, when the crowds went home, Jesus often went up into the hills to pray to God. Sometimes he prayed all night. After one night of prayer, he gathered those who were following him and learning from him. He chose twelve men among these disciples to be his closest companions and helpers, calling them apostles. They were Peter, Andrew, James, John, Philip, Bartholomew (Nathanael), Matthew, Thomas, James (son of Alphaeus), Simon, Thaddaeus (Judas, son of James), and Judas Iscariot.

Blessings

MATTHEW 5–7

MOST OF THE time Jesus taught the crowds out of doors where there was plenty of space. He went to sit on the hills around Lake Galilee, and people would gather to listen. Many of the people listening to him were eager to hear his words for guidance to improve their lives. They were poor and hungry, and in need, and were seeking happiness. They thought riches would bring them happiness, but Jesus spoke to them about what it was like in God's kingdom.

"Blessed are those who know they are poor in spirit, for the kingdom of God is theirs.

"Blessed are those who mourn, for they will find comfort.

"Blessed are the humble, for the world will belong to them.

"Blessed are those who want to do right more than anything else, for they will be satisfied.

"Blessed are those who give mercy to others, for mercy will be given to them.

"Blessed are those with pure thoughts, for they will be with God.

"Blessed are those who work to bring peace, for they will be called the children of God.

"Blessed are those who are treated badly for doing good, for the kingdom of God is theirs.

"Blessed are those who face people who hurt and lie about them, because they follow me. Be glad for they have a great reward waiting for them in heaven."

Jesus explained further, "You are like salt. Salt stops food rotting and adds taste to food. You are going to stop God's world going rotten and make it good again. Live your life as a light for other people. Love not only your friends but also your enemies. Give to the poor secretly, for God knows you have done this.

"Do not fight back but turn and offer the other cheek. If anyone forces you to go one mile, then go with him two miles.

"Do not store money or buy lots of things and spend your life getting rich. Money and possessions can be stolen. Instead store up your treasure with God, by following God's way. No one can take this away from you.

"Do not worry about your life. There is more to life than food and clothing. Look at the birds flying overhead. They do not work or store food in barns, but God feeds them. You are more valuable to God than the birds. You cannot add any time to your life by worrying about it.

"Do not judge others and you will not be judged.

"In everything, do for other people the same things you want them to do for you. This is the meaning of God's Law given to Moses and the teaching of the prophets."

The Lord's Prayer

MATTHEW 6

JESUS ALSO TAUGHT the people how to speak to God in prayer, saying, "Do not try to impress people with your prayers but find somewhere quiet. Talk to God as a father. Your father knows the things you need before you ask for them.

"Pray in this way:

"Our Father in heaven, hallowed be your name.

"Your kingdom come.

"Your will be done, on earth as it is in heaven.

"Give us this day our daily bread.

"And forgive us our sins, as we forgive those who sin against us.

"And do not bring us to the test, but rescue us from evil.

"Ask," said Jesus, "and it will be given to you; seek and you will find; knock and the door will be opened for you."

The people marvelled at his words, and were eager to hear and see him as he went from town to town in Galilee.

The Centurion's Faith

Matthew 8; Luke 7

THERE WAS A leader of a Roman army, a centurion, living in the town of Capernaum. He respected the Jewish faith and had even paid for the building of the synagogue. His servant was very unwell, and the centurion was distressed to see him suffering so terribly. He had heard about Jesus and his power to heal in the name of the Jewish God. He believed that Jesus would be able to help his servant, so when Jesus entered the town, the centurion went to see him.

"Lord," the centurion said, "my servant lies at home unable to move, in great pain."

Jesus replied, "I will come to your house and cure him."

In answer, the centurion said, "Lord, I do not deserve one who is as great as you to enter my house. I know you only have to give the order, and my servant will be healed. For I am also a man with authority over soldiers and when I say to a soldier, 'Go!' he goes and to another, 'Come!' he comes."

Jesus was amazed that the centurion had such faith in him and trust in God. He turned to the crowd of Jewish people, saying, "Nowhere else in this whole country have I found a person with such faith in me. There will be many who have not been born as Jews who will join the kingdom of God."

Jesus turned to the centurion and said, "Go home. Your servant is healed just as you believed he would be."

At that moment, the centurion's servant was well again.

The Story of the Sower

MATTHEW 13; MARK 4

AS JESUS SAT one day beside Lake Galilee, a huge crowd gathered around him. He climbed into a boat so that he could be seen by all the people on the beach. He told them a story to help them understand what he was trying to teach them. Jesus knew a story would engage them.

"Listen! A sower went out to sow his seeds. He threw them everywhere. Some seeds fell on the path, and the birds came and ate them. Other seeds fell on rocky ground, where there was not much soil. The plants sprang up quickly, but when the sun came up, they withered and died as they had no roots. Other seeds fell among thorny plants. The plants grew but the thorny plants were stronger and choked them. Other seeds fell on good soil and these plants grew and produced an abundance of grain in different quantities."

Afterwards the disciples asked Jesus to explain the parable to them.

He said, "The seeds are the words I speak about God's kingdom. The evil one comes and snatches away what is sown in people's hearts. These are the seeds on the path. Some people hear my words and receive them joyfully, but they only follow this for a while for when troubles come, they fall away. These are the seeds on rocky ground. Some people hear the words, but the desire for wealth and being distracted by the cares of the world stops them from being fruitful. These are the seeds among the thorns. But those who hear my words about the kingdom of God and understand them become fruitful in different ways. These are the seeds on good soil."

Calming the Storm

Matthew 8; Mark 4; Luke 8

One evening after a day of speaking to the crowds, Jesus decided to travel across Lake Galilee to take his message to those living on the other side. He and his disciples took a boat and, as the trip would take a while, Jesus fell asleep in the stern. As they sailed across, a storm swept over the lake. The boat was tossed around by the strong winds, whipping up the waves, and it began to fill with water. The disciples were very frightened for they were in danger of drowning if the boat broke up and sank.

Petrified, they woke Jesus, crying, "Teacher, do you not care that we are in great danger?"

Jesus woke and stood before the storm.

"Peace! Be still!" he commanded the wind and the water.

Immediately, the storm stopped and the sea became completely calm.

Jesus turned to his disciples, asking, "Why are you afraid? Do you still not trust me?"

The disciples were speechless and in wonder at what they had seen Jesus do. They whispered to one another, "Who can this man really be that even the wind and the waters obey him?"

They sailed on, safely reaching the furthest shore. Instead of crowds, they saw a man screaming wildly and lurching toward them. He lived among the tombs because he had been banished from the

town as not even chains were able to stop him hurting himself. When the man saw Jesus, he ran toward him.

Jesus was unafraid, and commanded, "Evil spirit, come out of this man!"

The man dropped to his knees in front of him, shouting at the top of his voice, "What do you want with me, Jesus? I know you are the Son of the Most High God. Don't torment and punish me."

Jesus asked, "What is your name?"

"Legion," the man replied, "for we are many evil spirits."

Nearby on the hillside, there was a great herd of pigs feeding.

"Send us into those pigs," begged the evil spirits.

Jesus agreed and at once the whole herd of pigs ran wildly down the hill and fell into the lake. The men looking after the pigs were shocked and rushed into the town to tell everyone what had happened. When the people from the town came, they found the man washed, dressed, and calmly sitting, talking with Jesus and the disciples. The people were amazed but did not welcome Jesus and asked for him and his disciples to sail back. The man wanted to go with them, but Jesus gently told him to stay and tell others about what God had done for him.

"Little Girl, Get Up!"

Mark 5; Luke 8

A GREAT CROWD GATHERED around Jesus and his disciples as they stepped ashore once more after sailing back. One of the leaders of the synagogue, named Jairus, approached and fell at Jesus' feet, begging, "My daughter is dying. Can you come and lay your hands on her so that she will be made well again?"

Jesus went with him and a large crowd followed them, pressing in on all sides as they went through the streets. Suddenly, Jesus knew that he had healed someone.

"Who touched me?" he asked the crowd.

A woman came forward, trembling nervously. She told Jesus that she had been suffering for twelve years, but no doctor had been able to stop the bleeding that had been making her ill. Jesus had been her only hope and she had touched his cloak. Immediately the bleeding had stopped.

"Your faith has made you well," Jesus said to her. "Go in peace."

While he was speaking, people came from Jairus's house with news that his daughter had died. There was no need for Jesus to come and heal her. It was too late.

"Do not be afraid," Jesus said to Jairus, "only believe and she will be well."

When they came to the house, everyone was weeping and wailing because the little girl was dead.

Jesus told them, "Why do you cry? She is not dead but sleeping."

He entered the house, sending everyone outside except for Jairus, his wife, and Peter, James, and John.

As the little girl lay there, Jesus took her hand and said to her, "*Talitha koum*", which means "Little girl, get up!"

Immediately the girl got up and began to walk around. Jairus and his wife were overcome with amazement that their daughter was alive again.

"Give her something to eat," Jesus told them, "and do not tell anyone about this."

Feeding the 5,000

MATTHEW 14; MARK 6; LUKE 9; JOHN 6

JESUS AND HIS disciples needed a rest and were trying to seek a deserted place by boat, but the crowd followed them. Jesus had compassion for the people because they were like sheep without a shepherd. He began to teach them about the way of God's kingdom, and they listened intently. Now the day was nearly ended, and no one had eaten.

"This is a deserted place," the disciples said to Jesus. "Send them away to the villages to buy something to eat."

"No," said Jesus, "we must give them something to eat. How much bread do you have? Go and see."

Andrew found a young boy with five loaves and two small fish and brought the food to Jesus. But this would not be enough to feed so many people, he thought, for there were more than 5,000 in the crowd.

"Tell everyone to sit down on the grass," Jesus said.

Taking the bread and the fish, Jesus gave thanks to God, and then passed the food to his friends to give out to the people. To his disciples' wonder, everyone ate until they were full and satisfied. They gathered the leftovers, filling twelve baskets. The people murmured that Jesus must be a prophet to be able to do such things.

Jesus withdrew to be by himself, and the disciples went down to the lake and started to sail back to Capernaum. The lake became rough because of the strong wind. As they rowed, the disciples saw a figure walking on the lake, coming toward the boat. They were terrified, thinking it was a ghost. The figure was Jesus.

"It is I," he said. "Do not be afraid."

Peter answered, "Lord, if it is you, then command me to come to you on the water."

"Come!" Jesus said.

Peter stepped out of the boat and started walking on the water toward Jesus, but then he noticed the strong wind and became frightened.

He began to sink and cried out, "Lord, save me!"

Jesus immediately reached out his hand and caught him, saying, "Your faith failed you. Why did you doubt?"

Then together they climbed into the boat and the wind calmed.

The next day the crowd went to find Jesus.

He told them, "You are looking for me because you ate your fill of the bread. This food perishes, but God sends you bread from heaven so that you will never hunger. I am the bread of life. Believe in me and I will give you all that you need for the new life that lasts for ever."

On the Mountain

Matthew 16–17; Mark 8–9; Luke 9

"WHO DO THE people say I am?" Jesus asked his twelve friends one day.

"Some say you are John the Baptist, who was beheaded by King Herod," they answered, "but others think you are Elijah or one of the other prophets come back to life."

"Who do you think I am?" asked Jesus.

Peter answered, "You are God's promised king, the messiah, who is the Son of God."

Jesus was pleased for he could now tell his close friends about some of the things that lay ahead and prepare them.

"God's plan is for me to be rejected and killed, but three days after I will be raised to live again. If anyone wants to follow me," Jesus continued, "let them be willing to suffer the same."

A short while later, Jesus took Peter, James, and John up a high mountain to pray. While he was praying, Jesus' appearance changed. His face shone like the sun and his clothes became a dazzling white. Two other figures appeared glowing brightly beside him. They were Moses and the prophet Elijah. They talked to Jesus about his death, which would soon happen in Jerusalem.

The three disciples were very tired, but they had stayed awake and saw this vision. A bright cloud came over them and a voice said,

"This is my Son, whom I love dearly. I am pleased with him. Listen to him!"

When the disciples heard this, they were terrified and fell to the ground, burying their faces.

Jesus came and touched them, saying, "Do not be afraid."

Looking up, the disciples saw that he was alone once more. Jesus told them not to tell anyone about what they had seen until he had died and been raised to life.

The Good Samaritan

Luke 10

ALTHOUGH JESUS HAD many friends, he also had enemies. Some of the religious leaders and the teachers of the Law, the Levites, were jealous and felt threatened by how popular Jesus had become. In particular, the Pharisees hated Jesus and what he was telling the crowds, and they often tried to ask tricky questions. Jesus always had an answer and often used the opportunity to tell the people stories to show how they should behave.

"Teacher," one of them asked Jesus, "what must I do to receive the new life?"

"What does God's Law tell you?" Jesus asked in reply.

"To love God with all my heart and soul, and with all my mind and strength," the man replied. "And to love others as much as I love myself."

"You are right," agreed Jesus. "Do this and you will have life."

"But what does it mean to love other people?" the man asked.

Jesus told this story.

"A Jewish man was on the road from Jerusalem to Jericho when robbers attacked and robbed him. He was left beaten and helpless on the road. After a while a priest came by, but when he saw the wounded man, he passed by on the other side of the road.

"A Levite also came past and he did not stop to help either. But a Samaritan came past and stopped when he saw the injured man. He cleaned and bandaged his wounds, and gently lifted the man onto his donkey and took him to the nearest inn to take care of him.

"The next day he had to leave but he gave the innkeeper some money, saying, 'Take care of him, and when I return, I will pay more for whatever you spend.'"

The crowd was surprised because the Samaritan had done this for a stranger and a foreigner, and Jews were not supposed to like people from Samaria.

"Which of these three people showed love to another?"

"The one who was kind to the wounded man," came the reply.

"Go," Jesus said, "and be like him."

The Rich Man and the Poor Man

Luke 16

The Pharisees saw wealth as a sign of success, and they showed very little compassion toward the poor people. They were proud, seeing themselves as more deserving of a position in God's kingdom than everyone else. Jesus tried to show and tell them that God knows what is in their hearts.

"There was a rich man," he told them, "who was dressed in fine clothes and feasted on plenty of food every day. At the gate to his fine house, there was a poor man named Lazarus, who was covered in sores and had nothing to eat. The poor man died and was carried by angels to be with Abraham in heaven. The rich man also died but he was buried and tormented.

"Looking up, he saw Abraham with Lazarus and called out, 'Father Abraham, pity me and send Lazarus to cool my tongue with water.'

"But Abraham replied, 'Remember during your lifetime you received your good things, and Lazarus did not receive anything, but now he is comforted and you suffer. There is also a great chasm between us that no one can cross.'

"The man said, 'Then I beg you to send Lazarus to my five brothers to warn them.'

"Abraham replied, 'They have God's Law given to Moses and the words of the prophets. They should listen to them.'

"'But,' the man said, 'they won't listen. Only if someone goes to them from the dead will they repent.'

"Abraham replied, 'If they do not listen, then they will not be convinced even if someone rises from the dead.'"

The Pharisees did not accept the warning message that Jesus was giving them. Instead their hatred of him grew.

The Least and the Lost

Matthew 18; Mark 9; Luke 15

As the disciples spent more time with Jesus, they had many questions for him as well.

"Who is the greatest in the kingdom of heaven?" they asked.

Jesus beckoned a child to come and be among them.

He said to his friends, "Truly, unless you become small like children, you will never know God's greatness. Whoever sees others more important than themselves like this child does is the greatest in God's kingdom. Whoever welcomes others as children of God in my name receives me into their hearts."

Jesus wanted to explain to them what their role was to be, making sure that they helped people find their way back to God.

"What do you think?" he asked. "If a shepherd has a hundred sheep, and one of them goes astray, the shepherd leaves the ninety-nine on the mountain and goes in search of the one that is lost. When he finds it, the shepherd rejoices and lifts it on his shoulders and returns home to celebrate with his friends."

Blessing the Children

Matthew 19; Mark 10; Luke 18

One day, some mothers brought their young children to be blessed by Jesus. Jesus was very busy talking to the crowd and the disciples thought he was too tired to be troubled by children. They told the mothers to take their children away, but Jesus overheard them.

"Do not stop them," Jesus told his disciples. "Let the little children come to me."

As the children came to him, he took them into his arms.

"The kingdom of heaven belongs to those who are the children of God," he said.

He blessed each child before continuing his way. The disciples wondered at Jesus' words and actions. Jesus regarded very important people, like the Pharisees, not to be important at all, and instead he would spend his time with mothers and children.

The Last Will Be First

MATTHEW 20

THE DISCIPLES HAD left everything to follow Jesus. Life was tough for them and Jesus had warned that they may suffer, too. One day, Peter asked, "What will be our reward?"

Jesus reassured him, "Truly, when I sit in glory, you who have followed me will also sit on twelve thrones. Everyone who has given up their comforts to follow me will receive new life. But many who are first will be last, and the last will be first.

“For the kingdom of heaven is like a landowner who set out early in the morning to hire workers for his vineyard. After agreeing with them the usual daily wage, they began work in the vineyard. About nine o’clock the landowner saw other workers standing idle in the marketplace and hired them, agreeing to pay them what is right. The landowner hired workers at noon and again at three o’clock in the afternoon. Again, at five o’clock, the landowner found others standing around for they had not found work all day, and so he hired them to work in his vineyard for the remaining hours of the day.

“When evening came, the landowner told the manager to call in the workers and pay them, beginning with the last to be hired. When those hired at five o’clock came, each of them received the usual

daily wage. Those who had worked all day saw this and thought they would receive more, but they were given the usual daily wage just like all the other workers.

"They grumbled to the landowner, saying, 'The last workers you hired worked for only one hour, and you have treated them equal to us who have toiled all day in the scorching heat.'

"The landowner replied, 'Friends, I am not doing you any wrong, for you agreed to work for the usual daily wage. I choose to give the same to the last who were hired. Am I not allowed to do this with the money that belongs to me? Or are you envious because I am generous?'

"So, the last will be first, and the first will be last."

Martha and Mary

Luke 10; John 11

Jesus and his disciples continued to tour the country. In some places they were accepted and in other places the people hastened them away.

In the village of Bethany, just two miles from Jerusalem, there lived a woman named Martha, who welcomed Jesus into her home. She had a sister named Mary, who came and sat at Jesus' feet, listening to his words. Martha was distracted by all the jobs of cooking and cleaning that she had to do. She was annoyed that her sister did not help.

Martha went to Jesus and said, "Tell my sister to come and help me."

But Jesus replied, "Martha, Martha, you are worrying and are distracted by too many things. There is only one thing you need to do. Mary is right to listen to me while she can."

Mary and Martha also had a brother named Lazarus, and whenever Jesus went to Jerusalem, he often stayed with them. One day, the sisters sent a message to Jesus that Lazarus was very ill. They

knew Jesus loved him and expected him to come straight away, but instead he stayed away for he knew God had a special purpose in this.

After waiting two days, Jesus then told his disciples that he was setting out. His disciples warned him that it was not safe to go toward Jerusalem because he had too many enemies there. But Jesus knew this was the right time. His disciples set out with him, fearing for their lives, too.

"Lazarus, Come Out!"

John 11

When Jesus arrived in Bethany, Lazarus had been dead for four days. He had already been wrapped and laid in the tomb. Martha went to meet Jesus.

"Lord, if you had been here my brother would not have died," she cried.

"He will live again," Jesus comforted her.

"I know he will, when God brings all the dead back to life at the resurrection on the last day," she answered.

Jesus said to her, "I am the resurrection and the life. Those who believe in me, even though they die, will live. Do you believe what I say?"

"Yes, Lord," Martha replied, "you are God's promised king, the messiah, the Son of God."

Mary and all their friends came and joined them, weeping, and Jesus wept, too. No one could understand why he had not come sooner to heal his friend.

Jesus went to the tomb, which had a stone rolled in front of its entrance.

"Take away the stone," he ordered.

Martha protested, "There will be a terrible smell from his body."

"Did I not tell you that if you believe, you will see the glory of God?" Jesus said.

The stone was taken away, and Jesus prayed. Then in a loud voice, he called, "Lazarus, come out!"

Lazarus appeared out of the tomb, still bound in the strips of cloth that were wrapped around dead bodies.

"Unwrap him, and let him be free," Jesus said.

Everyone watched in wonder, and many believed that Jesus had been sent to them by God.

The Expensive Perfume

John 12

When the Pharisees and the chief priests in Jerusalem heard what had happened at Lazarus's tomb, they knew they had to stop Jesus. They feared that the Romans would see the people stirred up and suspect a rebellion. The Romans would destroy the Temple and their nation. So the priests began planning to put Jesus to death.

The time of the Passover festival was near, and many from the countryside journeyed to Jerusalem to visit the Temple and celebrate. They remembered Moses leading the people of Israel out of slavery in Egypt with God's guidance. The chief priests and the Pharisees wondered if Jesus would be among them, so they gave orders that anyone who knew where Jesus was should let them know so that he could be arrested.

Jesus and his disciples had remained away from the crowds, but six days before the Passover, they came to Bethany and stayed at Lazarus's home. Martha served a fine dinner for them. Then Mary kneeled before Jesus and unbraided her hair. Everyone fell silent as she took some expensive perfume, poured it over his feet, and wiped them with her hair.

Judas Iscariot was horrified, and scolded her, saying, "Why was this expensive perfume not sold and the money given to the poor?"

"Leave her alone," Jesus told him. "Mary bought it to keep for the day of my burial. The poor will always be with you, but you will soon not have me with you."

Disgruntled, Judas fell silent.

The Triumphant Entry

Matthew 21; Mark 11; Luke 19; John 12

Jesus knew that the time had come to complete God's purpose and to enter Jerusalem to fulfil the events that the prophets foretold. He sent two of his disciples into a village ahead.

"You will immediately find a donkey with its colt tied up," he told them. "Untie them and bring them to me. If anyone asks about what you are doing, just say, 'The Lord needs them.'"

The two disciples did just as Jesus asked. They laid their cloaks on the young donkey, and Jesus climbed on and continued his journey into Jerusalem. The disciples went with him.

The road into Jerusalem was full of people, who recognized Jesus. They knew about all he had said and done, showing God's power. Full of excitement, they began to cheer. Some laid their cloaks on the road, like a carpet for a royal king. Others cut branches from the palm trees and began to wave them and lay them on the road as well.

The people and Jesus' disciples shouted joyfully, "Hosanna! Blessed is God's promised king! Praise God!"

As the jubilant procession entered the city gates of Jerusalem, the people inside the city wondered what was going on. The people from the countryside told them about Jesus. Watching on, the Pharisees knew that what they had been afraid of – Jesus stirring up the people – was now happening. But Jesus had come humbly on a donkey and peacefully, not marching in as a leader on a fine horse leading a rebellion.

At the Temple

Matthew 21; Mark 11; Luke 19

Jesus dismounted and led the way to the Temple. As he entered the courtyard, he was horrified to see what was happening. There were traders selling pigeons and doves for offerings and moneychangers giving out the special Temple coins, but they were cheating and taking more money from the people who had come to worship God.

Jesus became angry and overturned the tables, declaring, "God's Temple is a place of prayer, but you have made it into a robbers' den."

The people gathered around Jesus in the Temple. Blind and lame people came to see him, and he cured them. The chief priests and the teachers of the Law watched with increasing anger. Jesus had to be stopped.

Over the next few days, Jesus came to the Temple and taught the people about God's kingdom. He told his meaningful stories and the people listened eagerly, astounded by his words. The chief priests and elders challenged him about his authority to teach the people, and in return he challenged how they did not practice what they taught about God's Law. They were hypocrites! Jesus explained what would happen at the end of times spoken about by Moses and the prophets when the messiah comes in glory, and the dead who believe in him are raised to new life, known as the resurrection.

Two days before the Passover, the chief priests and elders gathered at the palace of the high priest, Caiaphas. They decided to arrest Jesus in secret and kill him. Judas Iscariot, one of Jesus' twelve apostles, went to see them. He was angry and disappointed that Jesus had not led the people to rebel against the Romans.

"What will you give me if I betray him to you?" he asked.

They agreed to pay him thirty pieces of silver, and he looked for an opportunity to lead them to Jesus when there were no crowds.

The Last Meal

MATTHEW 26; MARK 14; LUKE 22; JOHN 13

ON THE EVENING of the Passover celebrations, Jesus gathered with his close friends in an upper room of a house in Jerusalem. The meal was prepared and laid out on the table. Before beginning, Jesus took a towel and poured water into a basin. Then he began to wash his disciples' feet and wipe them dry with the towel. The disciples were surprised as this was a servant's job.

As he sat down, Jesus told them, "I have set you an example to serve one another."

Jesus was sad for he knew he would not be with his friends for much longer.

"One of you will betray me," Jesus told them.

The disciples looked at one another, wondering who he was talking about.

Then John asked, "Who is it?"

"The one to whom I am giving this piece of bread," said Jesus, dipping a piece into the sauce and giving it to Judas.

"Go and do it quickly," Jesus told him, and Judas immediately went out into the night.

As they ate, Jesus took a loaf of bread, gave thanks to God for it, and then broke it to be shared around.

"My body is going to be broken like this bread," Jesus said. "I die for you, so remember me when you eat bread together."

Jesus then took a cup of wine, gave God thanks, and passed it around.

"Drink from this cup and remember me. This is my blood as an offering to take away everyone's sins so all will be forgiven. My death will mark a new covenant of peace between God and people.

"I am with you only a little longer," Jesus told his friends, "but I give you a new commandment to love one another, just as I have loved you. I go to prepare a place for you in my Father's house. If you love me, you will follow the things I have told you. I will not leave you on your own to continue my work, but God will send the Spirit of truth to be with you and guide you always."

The friends were full of wonder at his words and never forgot them.

Betrayal

Matthew 26; Mark 14; Luke 22; John 18

When the meal was over, Jesus went out into the night to pray. He walked to an orchard of olive trees on the hillsides overlooking Jerusalem called Gethsemane, and his disciples followed him.

On the way, Jesus warned his friends what would soon happen. "Tonight you will all leave me and hide away."

"I never will!" said Peter.

Jesus replied, "Before the cock crows at daybreak, you will have denied knowing me three times."

Peter could not believe that he would do this, and the others agreed that they could not deny Jesus.

Jesus took Peter, James, and John with him into the orchard, while the others waited, keeping watch.

"Stay awake with me," Jesus asked them, while he went a little further and kneeled to pray.

"My Father," Jesus called out to God, "if it is possible, save me from this great suffering and death. But I will do what you want."

Three times he prayed, and each time he returned to his three friends but always found them asleep. The third time he woke them, there were people approaching with glowing lanterns. The group of Temple guards from the chief priests and elders came with swords and clubs, and leading them was Judas. He went up to Jesus and kissed him, as a sign to show the guards who to arrest. Jesus did not run away or try to stop them.

Peter, though, drew his sword and struck the servant of the high priest, cutting off his right ear.

"Put away your sword," Jesus told Peter. Then Jesus touched the servant's ear and healed it.

He turned to the Temple guards, asking, "Why have you come with swords and clubs as if I were a criminal? You did not lay hands on me when I was in the Temple every day. But this is the time when darkness rules."

Denial

Matthew 26; Mark 14; Luke 22; John 18

The guards seized Jesus roughly and took him to the high priest's house. The disciples feared for their lives and ran off, except for Peter, who followed at a distance.

A woman at the entrance to the courtyard said to him, "You are one of the man's disciples."

But Peter replied, "I am not."

He went into the courtyard and stood around the fire, warming himself. The Temple guards and servants of the high priest were standing around as well. Again, he was asked, and he denied knowing Jesus.

A while later, yet another person said, "You come from Galilee. Surely you must know this man, Jesus."

Peter shook his head, saying, "I swear that I do not know him."

At that moment, the cock crowed, announcing the dawn. Beaten and bruised, Jesus was led out and crossed the courtyard. He looked at Peter, and Peter remembered his words and he wept.

Sentenced to Death

Matthew 26–27; Mark 14–15; Luke 22–23; John 18–19

The Jewish council of elders, chief priests, and teachers of the Law gathered at the beginning of the new day. Jesus came before them as a prisoner on trial. Witnesses came forward to tell stories about what Jesus had said and done, but none of them agreed with each other. The council needed evidence before they could put Jesus to death. Jesus was silent.

Then the high priest said to him, "On oath, tell us if you are God's promised king, the messiah, the Son of God."

"You have said so," Jesus answered. "You will see me seated at God's right hand, coming on the clouds of heaven."

The high priest tore his clothes, announcing to the council, "Why do we still need witnesses? Jesus has claimed to be God's equal. This is blasphemy. What is your verdict?"

The council answered, "Guilty! He deserves death."

Jesus was bound and handed over to Pontius Pilate, the Roman

governor. The council needed Pilate's agreement to put Jesus to death. When Judas heard this, he was bitterly sorry for what he had done.

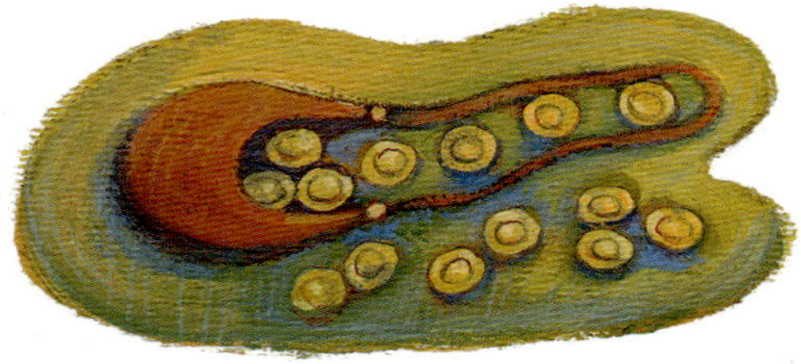

He went to the chief priests and gave them back the silver coins, saying, "I have betrayed an innocent man." Then he went away and hanged himself.

Jesus now stood before Pilate. The Jewish priests knew the governor would not sentence a man to death for blasphemy, so instead they accused him of causing trouble and treason.

Pilate asked Jesus, "Do you claim to be the king of the Jews?"

Jesus replied, "You say so."

Despite all the accusations, Jesus stayed silent. Pilate could see that there was no evidence, but the chief priests were insistent.

When Pilate heard that Jesus was a Galilean, he sent Jesus to the Jewish king, Herod, to be questioned. Again, Jesus stayed silent as Herod taunted him, but as Herod found no evidence for the sentence of death, Jesus was sent back to Pilate.

It was the custom at Passover for the Roman governor to release a prisoner. The crowd could choose between Jesus and a murderer named Barabbas. Stirred up by the priests, the crowd shouted for Barabbas to be released.

"Kill Jesus," the crowd shouted. "Crucify him!"

As Pilate sat on his judgment seat, a message came from his wife. It warned him to have nothing to do with Jesus for he was an innocent man. But the crowds kept shouting and he feared a riot.

So, in front of the crowds, Pilate washed his hands in a basin of water, saying, "I am not responsible for the death of this man. It is your doing."

Then Jesus was flogged and handed over to the Roman soldiers to be crucified.

At the Cross

Matthew 27; Mark 15; Luke 23; John 19

THE SOLDIERS PUT a scarlet robe on Jesus and twisted some thorns into the shape of a crown and pushed it down on his head, mocking him, saying, "Hail, King of the Jews!" Then they led Jesus through the city streets, as the crowds watched and jeered. Jesus had to carry the heavy wooden beam of a cross, but he stumbled and fell. A man in the crowds, named Simon of Cyrene, was ordered to carry the cross for him.

The place of crucifixion was outside the city walls in a place called Golgotha. Crucifixion was a terrible slow death hanging from a cross that the Romans used for criminals. The soldiers nailed Jesus' hands and feet to the beams of the cross and over his head was a sign, reading: This is Jesus, the King of the Jews.

The cross was lifted, and Jesus hung there in great pain, but he did not hate the soldiers.

"Forgive them, Father," he prayed, "they do not know what they are doing."

The people who passed by jeered at him, saying, "If you really are the Son of God, save yourself and come down from the cross."

The chief priests and elders mocked him, saying, "He saved others, but he cannot save himself."

On either side of Jesus were two criminals crucified with him.

One taunted him, but the other said, "We deserve to die, but this man has done nothing wrong. Remember me, Jesus, when you come as king."

Jesus replied, "I promise, today you will be with me in paradise."

Standing near the cross was Mary, Jesus' mother, and some of the women who followed Jesus. John stood with Mary.

Jesus spoke to John, saying, "Look after my mother for me."

At midday, the sun was blocked out and for three hours there was a strange darkness. Then Jesus cried out with a loud voice, "My God, why have you left me?"

Knowing he was near death, he whispered, "I'm thirsty."

A person nearby put a sponge filled with sour wine on a stick and gave it to him to drink. After receiving the wine, Jesus gave a loud cry, "It is finished!" and died.

At that moment, the curtain in the Temple split in two from top to bottom, and the earth shook violently. The soldiers and the centurion in charge were terrified.

"This man truly was God's Son," they marvelled.

The Stone Tomb

Matthew 27; Mark 15; Luke 23; John 19

A WEALTHY MAN NAMED Joseph from Arimathea, a secret follower of Jesus, went to Pilate and asked if he could take Jesus' body away for burial. Pilate agreed. To make sure that Jesus was dead, one of the soldiers pierced his side with a spear. Then they took his body down from the cross and gave him to Joseph.

Nicodemus, a Pharisee who secretly supported Jesus, brought myrrh and other spices, and they wrapped Jesus' body in long strips of cloth. They had to do this swiftly as it was soon to be sunset and the start of the sabbath, the day of rest. The women who loved Jesus followed them to a garden where there was a new tomb, and they watched as Jesus was laid there.

The chief priests and Pharisees remembered Jesus' claim that after three days he would rise from the dead, so they also went to Pilate to ask if their Temple soldiers could guard the tomb. They feared that Jesus' disciples would steal the body and tell others that he had been raised. Pilate agreed, and the guard rolled a great stone in front of the tomb, sealing the entrance, and kept watch.

Arisen and Alive!

Matthew 28; Luke 24; John 20

After the Sabbath, as the first day of the week was dawning, Mary Magdalene, Joanna, and Mary set off for the tomb, taking spices for Jesus' body. As they approached, the ground shook. A messenger sent from God in dazzling white came and rolled back the stone and sat on it. The guards were petrified and shook with fear, before running to tell the chief priests what had happened.

"Do not be afraid," God's messenger said to the women. "I know you are looking for Jesus, but he is not here. He is alive for he has risen from the dead. Look inside. This is where his body lay. Go quickly and tell his disciples, for they will see him again soon."

The women hurried to tell Jesus' friends, but they did not believe them. Peter and John went to the tomb to see for themselves. As they peered into the tomb, they were amazed to see just the linen cloths that had been around the body, neatly folded. They believed that Jesus' body had not been stolen but Jesus was alive.

Mary Magdalene, who followed them, stayed a while longer. She was shocked and weeping for she could not understand what had happened. She saw a figure and, thinking he was the gardener, asked, "If you have taken him away, please tell me where to find him."

"Mary!" came the reply.

She turned in surprise, and said, "Teacher!" for she knew at once that this was Jesus. She was filled with wonder and joy.

She rushed back to the disciples, saying, "I have seen Jesus."

The Walk to Emmaus

Luke 24

That same day, Cleopas and another of Jesus' followers were walking along a road to the village of Emmaus, outside Jerusalem. They talked about everything that had happened over the past few days and, as they were discussing, a stranger joined them.

"Why are you so sad?" the stranger asked.

"Are you the only person who does not know about what has taken place in Jerusalem?" Cleopas answered.

"Why, what's happened?"

"Have you not heard about Jesus of Nazareth?" Cleopas replied. "He was a great teacher and did amazing work in God's name. We hoped that he was God's promised king, but he was put to death on Friday. Then this morning some women went to his tomb and found his body gone, and God's messenger told them Jesus was alive."

"Why are you so surprised?" the stranger asked. "Don't you know that the messiah would suffer death and then enter into his glory?"

Then the stranger went on to explain how Moses and the prophets had foretold these events. As they came near the village, they invited the stranger to stay and eat with them as it was nearly dark. When the meal was ready, the stranger took the bread, gave thanks to God, broke it, and shared it with them. Immediately, the friends knew it was Jesus, but then he vanished. Excited, they hurried back to Jerusalem to tell Jesus' disciples about this wonderful experience.

Doubts and Belief

Luke 24; John 20

THAT EVENING, AS the disciples and other followers were together talking about what had happened, Jesus came and stood among them.

"Peace be with you," he said.

They were startled and afraid for Jesus stood before them and yet the doors were locked. They thought they were seeing a ghost, but Jesus said to them, "Why are you doubtful? Look at the marks of the nails on my hands and pierced feet. Touch me and see that I am real."

The disciples were full of joy but could hardly believe that it was true.

"Is there anything to eat?" Jesus asked.

They gave him some fish and watched him eat it. There could be no doubt that Jesus was alive once more. Jesus explained how everything that had happened was part of God's wonderful plan, as foretold in the words of God's Law, the prophets, and the psalms.

"God's promised king had to suffer and die," he said, "to then live again. Sin and death, separating people from God, has been conquered. All who believe and repent are forgiven and have new life. This is the good news to proclaim to people of every nation. You are witnesses of these things. Go out and tell them."

One of Jesus' disciples, Thomas, was not with the others that evening. He refused to believe what they were telling him.

"Unless I see and touch the mark of the nails for myself, I will not believe," he said to them.

A week later, the disciples were once again in the house, the doors shut, and Jesus came and stood among them.

"Peace be with you," he said. "Thomas, put your finger here on the marks on my hands and touch the sword wound in my side. Stop doubting and believe."

Thomas did not need to look or touch, for all doubts were gone.

"You are my Lord and my God," he said.

"You believe because you have seen me," Jesus said. "Those who have not seen me but still believe and trust me are blessed."

Breakfast on the Beach

John 21

Over the next few weeks, Jesus appeared to many of his followers. His friends left Jerusalem and returned to Galilee. One night, Peter, John, and some of the others went fishing, but they caught nothing. As dawn broke, a figure appeared on the shore.

"Have you caught any fish?" the man shouted to those in the boat.

"Nothing at all," they replied.

"Throw the net out to the right side of the boat," the man told them.

They did as he suggested and caught so many fish that they were unable to haul it in.

"It's Jesus!" John said to Peter.

Immediately, Peter jumped into the water and swam to see him. Jesus had prepared a fire on the shore and when the boat arrived,

they cooked some of the fish for breakfast together. Jesus took the bread he had brought and shared it around. After breakfast, Jesus and Peter talked.

"Do you love me?" he asked Peter three times.

"Yes," said Peter each time, "you know I love you."

"Take good care of my followers," Jesus said to him.

Peter knew that he had been forgiven by Jesus for denying him. God had special work for Peter to do that would eventually lead to his death.

Return to Heaven

Matthew 28; Luke 24; Acts 1

FORTY DAYS WEEKS Jesus had risen, the time had come for him to return to his Father in heaven. The disciples had gathered on a mountain and Jesus was with them.

"Although I must leave you," said Jesus, "you will receive the power of the Holy Spirit to help you speak out about all that you have seen and heard. You are to tell the good news about who I am and what I have taught you to the people in Jerusalem, Judea, and Samaria, and to the whole world. Tell them that whoever trusts in me and is truly sorry for the wrong they have done will be forgiven. They will receive new life through me. And remember, I am with you always to the end of time."

As Jesus said this, he was taken up to heaven. The disciples gazed up as a cloud hid him from their sight. Suddenly two messengers from God dressed in white appeared, standing beside them.

"Why do you gaze upward?" they said. "Jesus has gone to be with God, but one day he will return."

The disciples returned to Jerusalem, praising and worshipping Jesus.

Wind and Flames

Acts 2

In the days following, Jesus' friends gathered in an upstairs room in a house in Jerusalem. They prayed together and talked about the Scriptures.

On the day of Pentecost, Jerusalem was full of Jewish people from many different countries, celebrating the beginning of harvest. Jesus' apostles were together. Suddenly there was the sound like a strong wind, filling the whole house. Flames of fire touched each of them.

The Holy Spirit of God filled them just as Jesus had promised. They began to speak in many different languages, ones they had not known or learned.

The crowds heard them and were amazed because the men were telling them about the wonderful things God had done in their own languages.

Peter spoke to the crowds, saying, "Let me tell you about Jesus of Nazareth. He showed the power of God through wonders and signs, but he was crucified by you. This was God's plan, for God freed Jesus from death and raised him to life. He sits in glory as God's promised king and God's Spirit has been sent so that everyone can see and hear about this. We are witnesses to this."

The people listening were shocked that they had put God's promised king to death.

"What can we do?" they asked.

Peter replied, "Ask God to forgive you. Begin a new life and be baptized in the name of Jesus. God will give you the Holy Spirit to be with you."

That day, 3,000 people became followers of Jesus.

In the Name of Jesus

Acts 3–4, 12

EVERY DAY, JESUS' apostles and the new followers met at the Temple to pray and praise God. The apostles told them about what Jesus taught and shared the breaking of bread to remember him. What money the people had, they shared.

One day Peter and John went to the Temple. At the gate, they passed a man who had been unable to walk all his life. He was begging for money.

Peter spoke to him, saying, "I have no money to give you, but I can give you something more valuable. In the name of Jesus, stand up and walk."

Peter put out his hand to help the man, and immediately the man felt strength flow to his feet and ankles. Jumping up, he began to walk and entered the Temple, leaping for joy and praising God. The people around were full of wonder at what had happened to him. The priests of the Temple were angry though. They did not like Jesus' friends telling everyone that Jesus was risen from the dead and now they had made a lame man walk. So, they sent the Temple guards to arrest Peter and John.

The next day they appeared before the Jewish council of priests, elders, and teachers of the Law.

Caiaphas, the high priest, asked, "By what power were you able to heal the lame man?"

Peter and John knew their lives were in danger, but the Spirit gave them strength to speak truthfully.

"The man is healed by the power of the name of Jesus, who has become the cornerstone of God's kingdom," they said.

The council were amazed by their boldness. They wanted to stop the news of this spreading, so they ordered Peter and John not to speak or teach about Jesus again.

"Is it right to do what you tell us, or what God tells us?" Peter and John answered bravely. "We cannot stop speaking about the things we have seen and heard."

The council threatened them but had to let them go free. Peter and John went straight to their friends and reported what had happened. They began to pray, asking God not to keep them safe but to help them speak out boldly.

Many people in Jerusalem and the towns around came to hear the friends of Jesus. They brought those who were ill to be healed. Many of them believed what the disciples were saying about Jesus and became followers. The high priest ordered Jesus' friends to be arrested by the Temple guards and imprisoned. But during the night, an angel opened the prison doors and led them out. The next day, the priests were amazed to see them again teaching in the Temple.

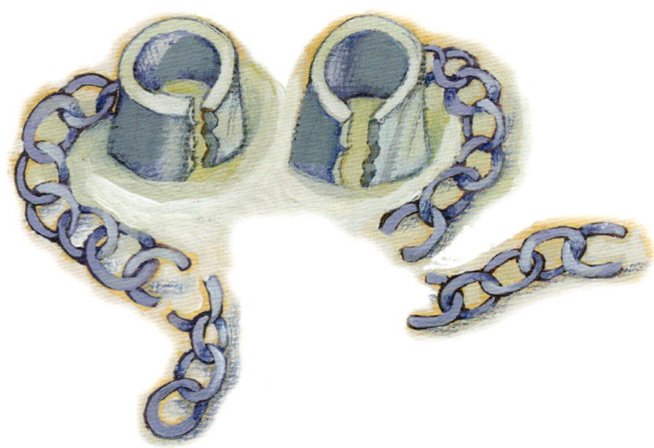

Brave Stephen

Acts 6–7

As the community of Jesus' followers grew, seven men were chosen to help resolve any disputes, such as the fair distribution of food among the poor widows of Jerusalem each day. One of these men was Stephen, who was a great speaker full of God's love and wisdom, and the crowds were eager to listen to him and see him perform miracles. He was arrested and brought before the Jewish council, falsely accused of speaking against Moses and God. At his trial, Stephen spoke to them about the history of Israel – about Abraham, Isaac, Jacob, Joseph, and Moses.

He reminded them about the times when the Israelites had turned away from God and worshipped idols and killed the prophets who spoke about the coming of God's promised king. Then he accused the council of being worse than their ancestors for they had betrayed and murdered him. The council were angered by what Stephen had said, but at that moment Stephen saw a vision.

"Look!" he cried out. "I see the heavens opened and Jesus standing at the right hand of God."

The council were furious and dragged him out into the city's streets and threw him to the ground outside the city walls. Then they hurled stones at him.

"Lord Jesus," Stephen prayed, "I give you my spirit. Don't hold this crime against them."

Then he died.

Good News Spreads

Acts 8

A MAN NAMED SAUL was watching the stoning of Stephen. He did not throw stones, but he approved of the killing of a follower of Jesus. Saul was a Pharisee, born far away in the trading city of Tarsus, but had studied God's Law in Jerusalem. After Stephen's death, he set about finding and imprisoning followers of Jesus. The followers were scattered throughout the countryside.

One of the apostles, Philip, went to Samaria, began to tell people there about Jesus, and healed those who were suffering. Many came to believe in Jesus and were baptized.

One day a messenger from God sent Philip to the Gaza road. An official from the court of the queen of Ethiopia was returning home in his carriage after visiting Jerusalem to worship. As he journeyed, the Ethiopian was reading aloud the words from the prophet Isaiah. Philip heard this and rushed over to the carriage.

"Do you understand what you are reading?" Philip asked.

"How can I," the official replied, "unless someone explains it to me?"

And he invited Philip to sit beside him and they chatted about the passage, which foretold the death of Jesus. Philip told him the good news about Jesus and the official wanted to become a follower. So they stopped by some water and Philip baptized him. As the official went on his way back to Ethiopia, Philip went on to other towns to speak of the good news.

A Blinding Light

Acts 9

Meanwhile, Saul the Pharisee was determined to find and arrest followers of Jesus. He asked permission from the high priest if he could travel to the city of Damascus. As he approached the city, suddenly a blinding light flashed around him. He fell to the ground and heard a voice calling his name: "Saul, Saul, why do you persecute me?"

"Who are you, Lord?" Saul asked.

"I am Jesus, whom you are ill-treating. Get up and go into the city, and you will be told what to do."

The men with Saul were speechless, for they could hear the voice as well. Saul got up from the ground, but he was blind. The men took him by the hand and led him into Damascus. For three days, Saul neither ate nor drank, and remained blind.

There was a follower of Jesus in Damascus named Ananias. God appeared to him in a vision, saying, "Look for a man named Saul, who is staying in a house in Straight Street. In his prayers, he has seen you lay hands on him so that his sight will return."

"Lord, this man has done terrible things to Jesus' followers in Jerusalem," Ananias answered. "He's come here to arrest us."

God said, "I have chosen this man to take my message to the nations of the world. I will show him all that he must suffer for the sake of my name."

So Ananias went to Saul and laid hands on him, saying, "Brother Saul, Jesus appeared to you and he has sent me here so that you may see again and be filled with the Holy Spirit."

Immediately, Saul's sight was restored and he was baptized, for his life would belong to Jesus from now on. He stayed with followers of Jesus and went to the synagogue to proclaim Jesus as God's promised king. Those who heard him speaking were full of wonder as they could not believe he was the same man who had previously imprisoned Jesus' followers. Saul's words were powerful and amazed them.

Before long, the Jewish people were planning to kill him. So one dark night, his new friends lowered Saul from the city wall in a basket so that he could escape and return to Jerusalem.

"Tabitha, Get Up!"

Acts 9–10

The apostle Peter was visiting the scattered groups of Jesus' followers. He journeyed from the towns of Lydda to Sharon and then on to Joppa. He talked about knowing and following Jesus. In Joppa, there was a follower of Jesus named Tabitha, also known as Dorcas. She had devoted her life to doing good works for others in need, making tunics and other clothes. But she became ill and died. Her body had been washed and laid in an upstairs room. Two men were sent to ask Peter to come to her.

Peter returned with them and then asked to be left alone with her. He kneeled and prayed, before turning to the body and saying, "Tabitha, get up!"

Tabitha opened her eyes and, seeing Peter, she sat up. News that Tabitha was alive spread around Joppa, and people believed in Jesus.

Peter stayed a while with a leather-worker named Simon in a house by the sea. A few miles away at Caesarea, there was a centurion named Cornelius. Although a soldier in the Roman army, he respected the Jews and their God, and gave generously to the poor. He also prayed to God every day but knew he could never hope to be a Jew and therefore one of God's people.

One afternoon at three o'clock, Cornelius had a vision, seeing a messenger from God who said, "God has heard your prayers. Send for Peter."

The next day at noon while lunch was being cooked, Peter prayed, falling into a trance. A large sheet was lowered from heaven. In it were all kinds of animals, some of which were on the list of "unclean" food that no Jew would eat as God's Law forbade it.

A voice said, "Get up, Peter. Kill and eat."

Peter replied, "I have never eaten anything unclean."

The voice said, "God has made them clean."

Three times this happened. Peter was greatly puzzled by his vision, but at that moment Cornelius's messengers appeared.

The next day, Peter went with the messengers to Cornelius's house. When Peter met Cornelius, he understood God's message.

"God treats everyone alike," he told the room full of Jews and non-Jews. "In every country, anyone who believes and follows God's ways is accepted by God."

The Holy Spirit fell upon everyone who was listening, and Cornelius and others were baptized.

Paul's First Journey

Acts 13–14

God's plan was for the good news about Jesus and God's kingdom to spread further. Saul, now known as Paul, and Barnabas were chosen to set out across the Mediterranean Sea. They visited the island of Cyprus before continuing on to towns and cities in what is now Turkey.

They always went to the synagogues first to tell the Jewish people the good news, but many would not listen. Paul and Barnabas spoke out boldly and many other people in the towns were glad to hear their teachings and believed. Often the Jews stirred up trouble and Paul and Barnabas had to move on swiftly, but they chose people to lead each new church group once they had left.

In the town of Lystra, there was a man who could not walk, who was listening to Paul intently. Paul could see that he had faith and said in a loud voice, "Stand upright."

The man sprang up and began to walk. The crowds were amazed and thought Paul and Barnabas to be two of the ancient Greek gods, Hermes and Zeus. The priest of the temple of Zeus brought oxen and garlands to the town's gates, and the crowds wanted to offer sacrifices to them.

Paul and Barnabas hastily told them that they were mortal just like them and tried to tell them about the God of heaven and earth. But trouble was stirred up and Paul was dragged out of the city, and only the followers of Jesus protected him, saving him from death. On their return, Paul and Barnabas were sent to Jerusalem to report on all that had happened.

New Disciples in Greece

Acts 16

Before long, Paul set off again, journeying this time with Silas. As they passed through the town of Lystra, a young follower named Timothy joined them for a while. He was son to a Jewish mother and a Greek father. He was well regarded by other believers in the town and Paul had much to teach and encourage him as a new disciple. He later became the bishop of Ephesus and Paul wrote letters of guidance and encouragement to him and the church there.

Paul was wondering where God would lead them, and one night he received a vision. A man from a region called Macedonia was calling out to him, "Come to Macedonia and help us."

So Paul and Silas, and also a doctor named Luke, set sail, arriving in the city of Philippi. A few days later it was the sabbath, so they went outside the city gates to the river, which they had heard was a place where the Jewish people prayed. There was a group of women gathered there.

Paul began to speak to them about Jesus and all that God had done for them through him. Among the group was a wealthy businesswoman named Lydia. Her business was to dye purple cloth, which was produced from thousands of sea snails and was very expensive to make. The purple cloth could only be afforded by the Roman emperor and noble people. Lydia listened eagerly to Paul and became the first person in Macedonia to believe. She brought her whole household to the river to be baptized and then insisted that the men stay in her home.

The Night in Prison

Acts 16

In Philippi, there was a slave girl who had a spirit that could predict the future and tell fortunes. Her owners made a great deal of money by her fortune-telling. As Paul, Silas, and Luke went about the city, the slave girl followed them, crying out, "These men are servants of the Most High God, who will tell you how to be saved."

At first the men tried to ignore her but after many days, Paul was annoyed and turned to the girl, speaking to her spirit: "In the name of Jesus, come out of her."

Immediately the spirit left her. The slave girl's owners were horrified that she could no longer tell fortunes. They seized Paul and Silas and dragged them to the marketplace to stand before the magistrates of the city.

"These men are disturbing our city," the owners accused. "They are Jews and breaking our Roman laws."

The magistrates ordered them to be publicly beaten and thrown into prison. They were handed over to the jailer, who put them in the innermost cell with their feet fastened in chains.

Despite their treatment, Paul and Silas did not complain. Instead they prayed and sang songs of praise to God. The other prisoners listened to them, amazed at the joyful sound and words.

Suddenly in the middle of the night, an earthquake violently shook the whole city. The foundations of the prison were shaken, causing all the cell doors to be opened and everyone's chains unfastened. The jailer awoke and was horrified to find the prison doors wide open. He knew if any prisoner had escaped he would be put to death.

As he drew his sword to strike himself, Paul shouted to him, "Do not harm yourself, for we are all here."

The jailer called for lights to be brought and rushed into the prison to find Paul, Silas, and all the prisoners with broken chains around them. The jailer fell, trembling, at the feet of Paul and Silas in wonder at the mighty power of God.

"Sirs," he said, "what must I do to be saved?"

"Believe in the Lord Jesus," they replied. "You and your whole family."

The jailer brought them into his house and washed their wounds, as they told him and his household about Jesus. They were all baptized and then food was given to Paul and Silas as the household celebrated.

In the morning, the jailer received the news that Paul and Silas were to be released and leave the city peacefully and in secret. However, Paul sent word to the magistrates that they were both Roman citizens, and it had been unlawful to publicly beat and imprison them. The magistrates were horrified that they had treated Roman citizens in this way. They apologized, but asked them to leave the city. Paul and Silas collected their belongings from Lydia's house, encouraged the new believers, and departed.

Riots and Arrest

Acts 17–21; 1 and 2 Corinthians

PAUL AND HIS friends continued to travel around Greece. In Thessalonica, the Jewish people stirred up a mob to seek them out and attack them. Finally, Paul arrived in the great city of Athens, but he was saddened to see all the temples and statues of gods. There was an empty altar with an inscription saying, "To an unknown god."

Paul immediately began to tell the people about the one true God who created the world.

"The Lord of heaven and earth does not live in shrines made by human hands but gives all people life and breath and all things."

Many scoffed at his words, especially about the assurance to believers of being raised from the dead, but a few believed.

In the bustling city of Corinth, Paul made two new friends, a Jew named Aquila and his wife, Priscilla. They had recently journeyed from Italy as the emperor Claudius had ordered all Jews to leave Rome. Paul stayed with them, as they were also tentmakers, which had been his trade before becoming a Pharisee. Silas and Timothy joined him, and they taught the people of Corinth about Jesus, establishing another growing church there.

Later, Paul would write letters to the church in Corinth when there were arguments among them. He described "true love" shown by Jesus to the world and explained that each person belonged to the "body" of Jesus and had a different important role to play given

by God. One member could not be without another, so they should share in someone's suffering and rejoice in someone's success.

After a considerable time, Paul set sail once again, finally returning to Jerusalem. However, keen to strengthen the followers in the new churches, once more he set off on a third journey. He stayed a while in Ephesus and the number of believers grew. But a silversmith who made silver shrines of the Greek goddess Artemis saw that his business was dwindling and stirred up the traders against them. The city rioted and two of Paul's friends were attacked. Afterwards Paul continued to visit the churches in Macedonia and Greece before finally setting sail back to Jerusalem.

On his journey, Paul was told by believers that it would not be safe for him to go on to Jerusalem.

Paul said, "I am ready not only to be bound but even to die in the name of Jesus."

Paul was not long in Jerusalem before he was the cause of another riot. He went daily to the Temple and some of the Jews stirred up the crowds, accusing him of taking non-Jews into the Temple. This was strictly forbidden. Paul was dragged out of the Temple. The Roman soldiers arrived just in time to prevent the crowd beating him to death. He was arrested and taken to prison.

Sent to Rome

Acts 23–27

PAUL APPEARED BEFORE the Roman tribune, the Jewish council, and the Roman governor Felix to be questioned, and he used these opportunities to speak out about Jesus and his work for God. As he was a Roman citizen, Paul was protected from the plots and accusations against him by the Jews. He was still imprisoned two years later, when a new Roman governor, Festus, was put in charge.

Paul stood before him, saying, "I have done no wrong to the Jews as everyone knows, so I appeal to the emperor of Rome. That is where I should be tried."

Festus spoke to Agrippa, the king of the Jewish people, and Paul appeared before him to defend himself and tell of his life as a follower of God, including his experience on the road to Damascus. They decided that Paul had done nothing wrong to deserve imprisonment or death and should be freed, but Paul had appealed to the emperor so could not be released.

Paul was taken with some other prisoners onto a ship under the command of a Roman centurion and set sail for Italy. At various ports, they transferred from ship to ship. The wind was against them and this slowed their progress and winter approached. At the island of Crete, Paul advised the centurion that the voyage would be dangerous, but he listened instead to the pilot and owner of the ship, who advised that they should sail on.

Shipwrecked!

Acts 27–28

A violent storm stirred up and battered the ship. To try and get the ship under control, the sailors lowered the anchor, but they continued to drift and be tossed around. They threw cargo overboard and then, on the third day, all the ship's tackle. The storm continued and those on board began to give up hope. They had also been without food for a long time.

One night a messenger from God visited Paul, saying, "Do not be afraid, Paul. You must stand before the emperor. God will keep safe all those who are sailing with you."

Paul told those on board the ship about his vision, encouraging them to keep up their courage.

"I have faith in God," said Paul, "that it will be exactly as I have been told. But we will have to run aground on some island."

On the fourteenth night, the sailors spied a possible island, and as they came close dropped the anchors. Some tried to leave the ship, but Paul warned them not to. Just before daybreak, Paul urged everyone on board to eat something as it would help to keep up their strength. There were 276 people on board. Paul took bread, gave thanks to God, and broke it before eating.

In the morning they could see the island and spotted a bay with a beach. The sailors cast off the anchors and discarded them in the sea.

They loosened the ropes that tied the steering oars and then hoisted the foresail to the wind, so the ship began to head for the beach.

But the ship struck a reef, the bow stuck, and then the stern broke up by the force of the waves. The centurion prevented the soldiers from killing the prisoners because he wished to save Paul. Instead he ordered those who could swim to jump overboard first, and then the rest follow, holding onto planks and other pieces of the ship. Everyone reached land safely.

They spent the winter on the island, which was Malta, before setting sail once again to continue to Rome.

Paul's Letters

Acts 28; Philemon; 2 Timothy

In Rome, Paul lived in a house with a soldier guarding him. Local leaders of the Jews came to meet him, and Paul told them that he had done nothing wrong. He spoke to them about the kingdom of God, trying to convince them about Jesus by referring to the Law of Moses and the words of the prophets. Some were convinced, while others refused to believe.

Paul lived in Rome for two years, welcoming everyone who came to see him, and writing letters to the churches he had established in response to news and queries he received from them. He wrote to the Ephesians, telling them that followers of Jesus, who were Jews and non-Jews, were all joined as one body through Jesus, and were all citizens together in the household of God. He encouraged them to show humility and gentleness, and patience with one another in love, living in unity and peace of the Holy Spirit.

Paul wrote letters to the churches in Philippi and Colossae, full of guidance and encouragement about how to live as followers of Jesus. He wrote about how the Holy Spirit was changing them for the better in their new life in Jesus, clothing them with love as God loved them.

One of the letters Paul wrote was to Philemon, one of the leaders of the Colossian church. The letter was about a slave, Onesimus, who was known to Philemon and had run away from Colossae. Onesimus was now a companion of Paul's in Rome, having become a follower of Jesus and changed.

Paul was sending Onesimus back, for a slave belonged to his master in those days. However, Paul encouraged Philemon to welcome him, treating him not as a slave but as a beloved brother in Lord Jesus. Paul was also willing to pay for anything that Onesimus had done wrong or owed, eager that Philemon would voluntarily do this. Paul signed off his letters with final greetings from other followers with him, and a prayer of blessing, known as the grace.

Paul was released and continued his journeys, but four years later, he was imprisoned once again in Rome. He wrote to his friend Timothy in his final days, stating, "The time for me to leave has come. I have fought the good fight, and finished the race, keeping the faith. Now there is waiting for me in heaven a crown of righteousness, which the Lord – the only true judge – will give to me on that final day. And not only to me, but also to all who long for his coming."

John's Vision

Revelation 1–3

THE GOOD NEWS of Jesus had spread from Jerusalem to all over the Roman empire. Jesus' followers encouraged each other with letters, and many were killed for their faith. People longed for Jesus to return in glory as he had promised to his apostles. One of these was John, who was banished to the island prison of Patmos as he would not stop speaking about Jesus.

He was praying one day and received a vision. His vision began with a loud voice like a trumpet, instructing him, "Write in a book what you see and send the message to seven churches."

John turned around and saw a glorious figure of Jesus, dazzling in brilliant light from seven golden lampstands. He was clothed in a long robe with a golden sash across his chest. His head and hair were as white as snow. His eyes were like flames of fire, his feet were like shining bronze, and his voice was like the sound of a powerful waterfall. In his right hand he held seven stars, and from his mouth flowed a sharp, two-edged sword, and his face was like the sun shining with full force. So powerful and wondrous was the sight that John fell at his feet.

Jesus placed his right hand on him, saying, "Do not be afraid. I am the first and the last, and the living one. I was dead, but see I am alive for ever and ever. I hold the keys of death and the afterlife. Now write down everything that I tell you."

Jesus gave him messages for each of the seven churches: Ephesus, Smyrna, Pergamum, Thyatira, Sardis, Philadelphia, and Laodicea.

The Glory of Heaven

Revelation 4–6

After receiving the messages, John looked and saw a wondrous vision of heaven with an open door. The trumpeting voice spoke, saying, "Come up here, and I will show you what must take place in the future."

John was in heaven, standing before a glorious throne with God seated on it like glistening gems. Around the throne was an emerald rainbow and twenty-four other thrones with elders sat on them in white robes and golden crowns. Flashes of lightning and peals and rumbles of thunder came from the throne, and seven flaming torches burned in front, which were the seven spirits of God. A sea of crystal was also in front of the throne.

On each side of the throne were four living creatures – a lion, an ox, a human face, and a flying eagle. Each had six wings and were full of eyes in front and behind. They sang day and night, "Holy, holy, holy, the Lord God the Almighty, who was and is and is to come."

Each time the creatures gave praise and thanks, the elders fell before God and worshipped.

In the right hand of God was a scroll written on both sides, and sealed with seven seals, and a mighty messenger of God proclaimed, "Who is worthy to open the scroll and break the seals?"

There was no one found worthy, until a Lamb stood before them, looking as if it had been killed, and took the scroll. The four living creatures and the elders fell before the Lamb, singing a new song: "You are worthy to take the scroll and to open its seals, for by your blood you paid the price for God's people from every nation. You have made them to be a kingdom serving God, and they will reign on earth."

Then every creature in heaven and on earth, and under the earth and in the sea – all of them, sang, "To the one seated on the throne and to the Lamb be blessing and praise and glory and might for ever and ever!"

The Lamb then opened the seven seals one by one, and wondrous and terrifying events occurred. War broke out in heaven between Michael leading God's angels and the serpent-dragon with his army of angels. Finally the serpent-dragon was defeated both in heaven and then on earth. There was rejoicing in heaven and a great day of judgment.

The Wonder of a New Creation

Revelation 21–22

In his vision, John saw a new heaven and a new earth, for the first heaven and the first earth had vanished and the sea had disappeared. He saw the Holy City, a new Jerusalem, coming down from heaven like a beautiful bride clothed in riches for her husband. He heard a loud voice from the throne of God, saying, "See, this city is the home of God among the people. God has come to be with them and will wipe away every tear. Death and pain will be no more.

"Write this. See, I am making all things new. It is done! I am the Alpha and the Omega, the beginning and the end. I will give water to the thirsty as a gift from the spring of the water of life. My children will inherit all these things."

Then an angel carried John to a great, high mountain to more clearly see the Holy City, which radiated like a rare, sparkling jewel. He saw the new Jerusalem had a great, high wall with twelve pearl gates and at the gates twelve angels, and on the gates were inscribed the names of the twelve tribes of Israel. The wall of the city had twelve foundation stones adorned with every jewel, and on them were the twelve names of the Lamb's apostles. The wall was built of a sparkling gem named jasper, while the city was made from pure gold as clear as glass.

John could see the river of the water of life flowing from the throne of God and the Lamb through the middle of the city's street. On either side of the river was the tree of life bearing twelve kinds of fruit with leaves that bring healing. There was no temple as the throne of God and the Lamb were there, and there was no need of sun or moon, for God's glory was its light and the Lamb its lamp. The gates would never be shut by day, and there was no night. People would bring into the city the glory and praise of the nations.

Then the resounding voice of Jesus called to John, "See, I am coming soon!"

John wrote down everything that he had seen and heard in the wondrous vision, ending, "Amen. Come, Lord Jesus! Amen."

Index of People's Names

THE OLD TESTAMENT

Aaron 51–53, 58, 128
Abel 18
Abram/Abraham 24, 26–33, 50–51, 59, 128, 177–78, 219
Adam 15–18, 128
Adonijah 92
Ahab 98–102
Asher 35, 66
Azariah/Abednego 114–15, 117
Balaam 62–63
Balak 62
Bathsheba 91–92
Belshazzar 117
Benjamin 38, 44, 46, 66
Boaz 72–73, 80
Cain 18
Caleb 61
Cyrus 119
Dan 35, 66
Daniel/Belteshazzar 114–15, 117–18
Darius 117–18
David 80–82, 84–86, 90–93, 120, 128, 131, 134–35
Dinah 35
Ebed-Melek 112
Eli 74–75, 77
Elijah 98–100, 102, 171
Elimelek 71, 73
Elisha 100, 102–06
Enoch 18
Esau 32–33, 36
Esther 121–24
Eve 17–18
Ezra 120
Gad 35, 66
Gideon 69–70
Goliath 81–82
Hagar 28, 30–31
Haggai 120
Ham 18
Haman 122–24
Hananiah/Shadrach 114–15, 117
Hannah 74

Hezekiah 110
Huldah 111
Isaiah 110, 148, 220
Isaac 29–33, 50, 59, 128, 219
Ishmael 28, 30–31
Issachar 35, 66
Jabal 18
Jacob/Israel 32– 36, 38–40, 44, 46–48, 50, 59, 61, 128, 219
Japheth 18
Jeremiah 112–13
Jeroboam 96–98
Jeroboam II 107
Jesse 73, 80–82
Jezebel 98, 100–02
Joab 92
Jochebed 48
Jonah 107–10
Jonathan 79, 84–85, 90
Joseph 35, 38–44, 46, 47, 219
Joshua 61, 64–68
Josiah 111–12
Judah 35, 46, 66
Laban 33–36
Leah 34–35
Levi 35, 66
Lot 24, 26
Mephibosheth 90
Miriam 48
Mishael/Meshach 114–15, 117
Moses 48, 50–54, 56–61, 64, 93, 94, 128, 156, 171, 178, 187, 191, 208, 219, 239
Naboth 101–02
Naaman 105–06
Naomi 71–73
Naphtali 35, 66
Nathan 86, 92
Nebuchadnezzar 112–15, 117
Nehemiah 120
Noah 18, 20–21, 23–24
Obed 73, 80
Orpah 71
Rachel 34–35, 38
Rahab 64–66
Rebekah 32–33
Rehoboam 97–98
Reuben 35, 40, 66
Ruth 71–73, 80
Samuel 74–75, 77–81, 85

Sarai/Sarah 24, 26, 28–30
Saul 78–79, 81–82, 84–85, 90
Seth, son of Adam 18
Seth, son of Noah 18
Simeon 35, 44, 46, 66
Solomon 92–94, 96–97
Tubal-Cain 18
Uriah 91–92
Xerxes 121
Zadok 92
Zebulun 35, 66
Zechariah 120
Zedekiah 112–13

THE NEW TESTAMENT

Agrippa 236
Ananias 221, 223
Andrew 149–50, 154, 169
Anna 139
Aquila 233
Barnabas 226–27
Caiaphas 191, 217
Cleopas 208
Cornelius 225
Elizabeth 128–29, 131, 133, 145
Felix 236
Festus 236
Gabriel 128, 131
Herod 128, 140, 143, 171, 200
Jairus 165–66
James 149, 154, 166, 171, 195
James, son of Alphaeus 154
Jesus 126, 131, 133, 139–40, 143–44, 146–50, 152–56, 158–62, 164–66, 168–74, 177–82, 184–88, 190–93, 195–98, 200–02, 204–12, 214–21, 223–24, 226–27, 229–30, 232–33, 235–36, 239, 241–43, 250
Joanna 206
John (apostle) 149, 154, 166, 171, 193, 195, 202, 207, 211, 217–18
John the Baptist 128, 133, 145–46, 171
John (Revelation) 242–44, 248, 250
Joseph 131, 133, 134, 138, 139, 143, 144, 148
Joseph of Arimathea 204
Judas Iscariot 154, 187, 191, 193, 195, 200
Lazarus (poor man) 177–78
Lazarus of Bethany 184, 186–87

Luke (doctor) 228, 230
Lydia 229, 232
Martha 184, 186–87
Mary (Jesus' mother) 131, 133–34, 138–39, 143–44, 152, 202, 206
Mary of Bethany 184, 186–87
Mary Magdalene 206–07
Matthew 153–54
Nathanael/Bartholomew 150, 154
Nicodemus 204
Onesimus 241
Peter/Simon Peter 149–50, 154, 166, 170–71, 182, 195–97, 207, 211–12, 216–18, 224–25
Philemon 241
Philip 150, 154, 220
Pontius Pilate 198, 200, 204–05
Priscilla 233
Saul/Paul 220, 221, 223, 226–33, 235–39, 241
Silas 228, 230–33
Simeon 139
Simon (apostle) 154
Simon (leather-worker) 225
Simon of Cyrene 201
Stephen 219–20
Tabitha/Dorcas 224
Thaddaeus/Judas (son of James) 154
Thomas 154, 210
Timothy 228, 233, 241
Zechariah 128–29, 133, 145